From Me

To You

This Day

On the Occasion of

TOTAL FREEDOM

SAM O. ADEWUNMI

Foreword: Revd. Dr. Paul Jinadu

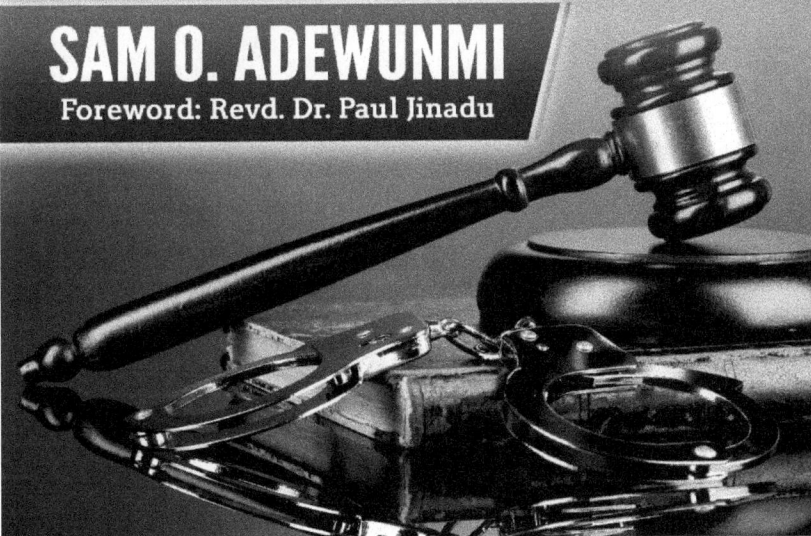

TOTAL FREEDOM

Sam O. Adewunmi

COVENANT PUBLISHING

TOTAL FREEDOM
Sam O. Adewunmi

Unless otherwise stated, all scripture quotations are taken from the Holy Bible, New King James Version (NKJV). Other versions cited are NIV, KJV, GNB, God's Word, BBE, MSG, LEB and NLT.

ISBN 978-1-907734-38-0
First Edition
First Printing November 2018

TOTAL FREEDOM
The following books are included in this anthology
- Turning Temptations Into Triumphs: **ISBN 978-1-907734-12-0** © February 2015 by Covenant Publishing
- Good Finish To Bad Start: **ISBN 978-1-907734-44-1** © January 2013 by Covenant publishing
- Your Basket, Kneading Bowl and Barn: **ISBN 978-1-907734-14-4** © November 2013 by Covenant Publishing

Covenant Publishing
samadewunmi@btinternet.com

Cover Design by Covenant Publishing Team
Sam O. Adewunmi's photo by David Adetoye
Published by Covenant Publishing
Printed in the United Kingdom

CONTENTS

DEDICATION

Dedicated to the love of my life, my
lovely Advanced Skilled Helper
OLUWATOYIN ADERONKE
"ADEMI", who is both God's
wonderful gift to me and my
personal overseer on my journey to
Total Freedom

FOREWORD

Some ministers write books because they feel it's their ministry. Others write because they want to be able to say they have written books, just like their peers. I feel this book, however, is written because the author has a vast knowledge of his subject. More importantly he feels a sense of compulsion to share his experiences and observation.

I would encourage you to read the book. For I have read the author, the man himself, over a period of 25 years as a member of our church and now member of its leadership. What he says is little compared to what he has seen. And he has seen a lot.

Paul Jinadu
General Overseer
New Covenant Church

BOOK 1

Turning Temptations Into Triumphs

God's Proven Strategies Against Satanic Devices

CONTENTS

Introduction

| Show Up, Step Up and Stand Up |

Had Adam known what you and I now know, he probably would have given more thought to his action. We know that what we do or omit to do knowing we are supposed to do might end up affecting four generations after us. Such knowledge was not available to Adam. The entire universe is suffering the consequences of Adam's wrong choices.

> *"For we know that the whole creation groans and labours with birth pangs together until now" (Romans 8:22).*

The question that must now be answered is this: What would it take to reverse this catastrophe? The answer is found in Romans 8:19. We need to come out of hiding. We need to show up, step up and stand up. We manifest His power when we stop hiding and begin to establish God's kingdom here on earth.

> *"For the earnest expectation of the creature waiteth for the manifestation of the sons of God" (Romans 8:19, KJV).*

God is looking for a remnant that will not deny Him or deny their faith. Showing up, stepping up and standing up means we would be bold to declare our allegiance to Him. It means we would be proud to be identified with Him. We may take an unpopular stance; however, it is better to stand with the One that matters at the end of the day. This is not only in our Churches. It is not in the apparels we wear or the music we sing, but out on the streets and in the market place.

The world needs to see us. They need to see a generation that is not in the kingdom business for their own benefits. They want to see a place where their children are safe at the hands of their ministers. They are looking for a place where their wives and daughters will not be abused; a place where their sons will not be molested.

The world is waiting for a people that will report to work on time, stay at work and complete their shifts; a people who would not call sick when they are okay and well enough to work; a people that will do beyond the expected, not in a bid to win man's approval but doing so as unto the Lord. When it comes to consistency, their employers are proud of them and when there is redundancy, they are the last to be considered.

The world is waiting for a people that when they say 'I do,' they really do. Not because it is fashionable to say 'I do' but because it comes from the depth of their being; those who would say, 'for better or worse,' and stay put, whether it is better or worse. We are talking about a generation that will look after their wives and their children, not shifting or shirking their responsibilities. The world is already too filled with individuals raised in single parent homes.

The world is waiting to see in us a huge river, gracefully moving in the might of the Holy Spirit – irresistible and unrelenting. Not a bunch of motionless cesspit of religious people or a shallow lake going nowhere, but a monumental river with an inconceivable current. The moment you become part of it, you are no longer your own but entering with reckless abandon, allowing the current of God to carry you to wherever He wishes.

The world is waiting to see a church that is not only physically growing but also a church that is holy and blameless, without spot or wrinkle. They are waiting for the manifestation of a church that is after the Lord's heart where race and gender differences are what make it whole and not what brings division. A church where every soul is significant; though the salvations of its individual souls are personal, the community is essentially one.

The world is tired of hypocrites; who says one thing but practice another. In the public, they are the nicest of people, but privately, they terrorise their families. They tell their children 'not-to' but do the 'not-to'; leaving them more confused. They wear nice clothes on Sunday but you cannot even recognise them as Christians on Monday through Saturday. In their closets, they watch immoral stuffs and read immoral junks.

People want to see those whose 'yes is yes', and 'no is no.' They are no longer interested in rhetoric but want to know what is on our minds even if it is at variance with their interests. Least, they can make up their mind if they want to join our camps. The time of pretence and lies are over. God is looking for a generation whose words can be counted on; on whose promises we can rely.

Until we show up, stand up and step up, we would continually be the laughing stock of a perishing world. Until we stop blaming the devil for our actions; giving him some recognition and taking responsibility for our mistakes, the church would not be taken serious.

The sacrifices may be high but the rewards are higher. Your friends may be doing it but you have to refuse to join in. And, if you stick with it, you shall surely rejoice. It may be popular to cheat but you prefer rather to go without; that is sacrifice and it shall not go unnoticed and unrewarded. After all, the bible says, you shall be perfect, established, strengthened and settled for your sacrifice. That's the promise of God.

> "But may the God of all grace, who called us to His eternal glory by Christ Jesus, after you have suffered a while, perfect, establish, strengthen, and settle you" (1 Peter 5:10).

It was tempting for Jesus to quit, yet He did not. It was easy to let go, but He refused. What did He do? He endured the pain, the agony, and the shame of the cross all because of us and the reward waiting to be claimed.

> "Therefore, since we are surrounded by such a huge crowd of witnesses to the life of faith, let us strip off every weight that slows us down, especially the sin that so easily trips us up. And let us run with endurance the race God has set before us. We do this by keeping our eyes on Jesus, the champion who initiates and perfects our faith. Because of the joy awaiting him, He endured the cross, disregarding its

shame. Now He is seated in the place of honor beside God's throne" (Hebrews 12:1-2, NLT).

It was worth it at the end. What would you have done? Say it loud and let the Lord hear you and let your neighbour be your witness.

In humility, I invite you to join me in declaring that it can be done. We can be faithful husbands, honest employees, disciplined disciples, trusted leaders, enviable dads, and good stewards. Oh yes we can!

The devil can be defeated. He can be beaten, squashed, and shamed. You can stand your ground and say 'No' to the devil and 'Yes' to God. Oh yes you can! It's not going to be a walk in the park but you would get there.

Welcome to freedom living. The journey starts here; I mean, in the next page.

TOTAL FREEDOM

Chapter 1

| **LIVING IN THE FEAR OF GOD** |

We celebrated the 200th year of the abolition of slavery in 2007 which related to physical liberation. Although slave trading is now illegal, and people may no longer be physically enslaved, they can be taken captive by so many other things. For example people may be incarcerated by debt.

> *"Poor people are slaves of the rich. Borrow money and you are the lender's slave" (Proverbs 22:7, GNB).*

Many people have gone into debt and because of that, they have become slaves to their lender. Until they have fully paid whatever was taken as loan, they will continue to work for the lender. It is very crucial that we do not get into debt so that we can fulfill God's plan for our lives without anything holding us back.

Although our physical and material lives are important, the most important area of life Christians have to seek deliverance and pay more attention is our spiritual lives. If you spend time profitably and do well economically but neglect your spiritual needs, you will eventually lose everything.

"Will people gain anything if they win the whole world but lose their life? Of course not! There is nothing they can give to regain their life" (Matthew 16:26, GNB).

You can have everything and yet possess nothing. Material success is not the ultimate goal one should seek in life. Spiritual fulfilment approved of God should be everyone's desire. So how can we redress ungodly desires? How can we refocus our gaze? How can this be done?

Living in the fear of the Lord will help us to avoid selling our future to the devil. Making sound moral judgement and choices will help us to avoid heartaches like those of Adam, Abraham and David. Our decisions will either make or mar our future. If we want a triumphant finish, we have to work on our moral choices.

People do not have to be in chains to be bound but can be in chains and yet are free. Not everyone in prison is bound, and not everyone on our streets is free. One may be physically free but emotionally, mentally, financially and morally bound.

Mr. Spurgeon once made a parable. He said, "There was once a tyrant who summoned one of his subjects into his presence, and ordered him to make a chain. The poor blacksmith – that was his occupation – had to go to work and forge the chain. When it was done, he brought it into the presence of the tyrant and was ordered to take it away and make it twice the length. He brought it again to the tyrant, and again he was ordered to double it. Back he came when he had obeyed the order, and the tyrant looked at it, and then commanded the servants to bind the man hand and foot with the chain he had made and cast him into prison.

"That is what the devil does with men," Mr. Spurgeon said. "He makes them forge their chain, and then binds them hand and foot with it, and casts them into outer darkness."

Friends, this is just what the drunkard, gambler, blasphemer, and every sinner is doing. Thank God, we can tell them of a deliverer. The Son of God has the power to break every one of their fetters if they will only come to Him.

I have counselled many believers who are addicts of pornography, lies, alcohol, or drugs of every kind. They are free but still bound. It is possible as a child of God to be held captive by the devil in particular areas. Many Christians refuse to admit that they are struggling with pornography, drinking or gambling addictions. Others are held captive by debt, immigration problems, failures and other limitations placed on them by choice or other people's negligence.

Many people quote what they do not fully understand. Here is a scripture commonly used.

> "If the Son therefore shall make you free, you are free indeed" (John 8:36, KJV).

Free from what? The answer is simple yet profound: free from the guilt, presence and penalty of sin but not the power of sin. I know this is hard to swallow. The text is talking about the first level of freedom, nothing more. Jesus was talking about Justification not sanctification. Justification sets you free from the guilt, presence and penalty of sin, but only Sanctification can set you free from the power of sin and that is the work of the Holy Spirit after conversion. Many are free from the presence of sin but not from its power. Even Apostle Paul had this struggle in his life. That was what he said in Romans 7:14-23. He was free from the presence of sin but not its power. He later found a way out through Sanctification.

On one of his European tours, the master magician and locksmith Harry Houdini found himself locked in by his thinking. After he had been searched and manacled in a Scottish town jail, the old turnkey shut him in a cell and walked away. Houdini quickly freed himself from his shackles and then tackled the cell lock. However, despite all his efforts, the lock would not open. Finally, ever more desperate but utterly exhausted, he leaned against the door, and it swung open so unexpectedly that he nearly fell headlong into the corridor. The turnkey had not locked it.

The Israelites left Egypt, but Egypt did not leave them. They crossed the Red (Reed) Sea but still had the Jordan to cross. They all perished in the wilderness save two, Joshua and Caleb. They were baptised in Moses but not in Joshua. They were justified but not sanctified. They negotiated their freedom with Pharaoh while they were in Egypt, but there was no one to negotiate with in the wilderness but their hearts. With the army of Pharaoh they conquered but of the battle of the mind they lost. It is in the ministry of the Holy Spirit, through Sanctification, that any solution can be found.

> "'... Not by might nor by power, but by My Spirit,'
> says the LORD of hosts" (Zechariah 4:6).

Those are free who are in prison, but have Jesus, and those are bound who reside in their home without Jesus. Freedom is not the absence of physical chains; it is the presence of Jesus. Everyone came to the earth, bound. They may appear on the outside to be free but, on the inside, they are bound, and only

Jesus sets men free. To be held captive is to be placed under restrictions within a boundary (physical or spiritual) against your will. Paul cried,

> "Oh, what a miserable person I am! Who will free me from this life that is dominated by sin?" (Romans 7:24, NLT).

> "Thank God! The answer is in Jesus Christ our Lord. So you see how it is: In my mind I really want to obey God's law, but because of my sinful nature I am a slave to sin" (Romans 7:25, GNB).

> Jesus said of Himself, "… I have come that they may have life (Zoe), and that they may have it more abundantly (perissos)" (John 10:10).

It is two-stage deliverance. Zoe is the life of God received at salvation. Perissos is the beyond measure life after salvation; the superior, superabundant, excessive life of God. A Christian may have 'zoe' but not 'perissos' because they have been held captive in an area. So Jesus came to proclaim liberty to the captives.

> "The Spirit of the Lord God is upon Me, because the LORD has anointed Me… to proclaim liberty to the captives" (Isaiah 61:1).

Slavery To Sin

Writing to Christians in Rome Paul penned this,

> "Surely you know that when you surrender yourselves as slaves to obey someone, you are in fact

the slaves of the master you obey – either of sin, which results in death, or of obedience, which results in being put right with God" (Romans 6:16, GNB).

Everything we do have consequences. What we are experiencing today are fruits of seeds previously sown and they in turn become seeds that may yield future fruits. If we serve Satan and become a slave to sin, it will lead to death. If we serve God and are His slave unto obedience, it leads to righteousness. That is just the way it goes. Our actions or omissions have their consequences. There is a wage, a payback. If we do not get the results now, wait and it will come. If we do not pay for it now, we may be paid for it. There is always a wage.

"For the wages of sin is death, but the gift of God is eternal life in Christ Jesus our Lord" (Romans 6:23).

Lots of people have paid the ultimate untimely price for a little indulgence – so to speak. Some have died of AIDS or STIs because they could not control their sexual appetites.

"Do not be deceived, God is not mocked; for whatever a man sows, that he will also reap. For he who sows to his flesh, will of the flesh reap corruption, but he who sows to the spirit will of the spirit reap everlasting life" (Galatians 6:7-8).

Generational Curses

Those who claim that there is nothing like generational curses lack understanding. It will take several pages to fully explain the ministry of deliverance. But let's do a one-paragraph crash course.

Generational curses are real. Demonic possession occurs in the realm of the spirit while demonic oppression occurs in the realm of the soul and the flesh. For an unsaved person, he or she can be both possessed and oppressed because the pronounced curse of the Old Covenant is active up to the fourth generation of the unsaved. When we become saved, our spirit is renewed but the soul and the flesh are not. Justification deals with the spirit in man but deliverance deals with the soul and flesh. The devil is unable to possess the believer, but he or she can be oppressed. When we cast out demons, we are dealing with the generational consequences of idolatry. As explained earlier, this is two-stage deliverance. Jesus raised Lazarus from the dead, but Lazarus remained bound until the disciples were instructed to lose him. A lot of Christians are alive but may be bound in certain areas of their lives. The rest is for another day.

The effects of sins committed may be felt up to the fourth generation. By one act of disobedience, you could have sold your children, grandchildren and great grandchildren and great-great grandchildren into slavery. In the same way, the effect of being obedient to God may last until the thousandth generation. By one act of love, you could have blessed a thousandth generation in your family. Which is better? Let me show you.

> *"You shall not make for yourself an idol in the form of anything in heaven above or on the earth beneath or in the waters below. You shall not bow down to them or worship them; for I, the LORD your God, am a jealous God, punishing the children for the sin of the fathers to the third and fourth generation of those who*

hate Me, but showing love to a thousand generation
of those who love Me and keep my commandments"
(Exodus 20:4-6, NIV).

David McCullough in his book 'Mornings On Horseback' tells this story about young Teddy Roosevelt: Mittie (his mother) had found he was so afraid of the Madison Square Church that he refused to set foot inside if alone. He was terrified, she discovered, of something called the 'zeal.' It was crouched in the dark corners of the Church ready to jump at him, he said. When asked what 'zeal' might be, he said he was not sure, but thought it was probably a large animal like an alligator or a dragon. He had heard the minister read about it from the Bible. Using a concordance, Mittie read him those passages containing the word ZEAL until suddenly, very excited, he told her to stop. The line was from the Book of John, 2:17: "And his disciples remembered that it was written, 'The ZEAL of thine house hath eaten me up'! People are still justifiably afraid to come near the 'zeal' of the Lord, for they are perfectly aware it could "eat them up" if they are not one of His. Our Lord is good, but He isn't safe.

You need not fear the zeal of the house of the Lord. Many people fear things or creatures of God rather than God. The only One you need to fear is God. The reverent fear of the Lord will prevent you from wanting to do what you know will offend Him. If you love someone, you will do all that is in your power not to offend them. So we fear God out of reverence for Him, not because He holds a long white cane waiting for us to go wrong so He can punish us.

One time many years ago, the king of Hungary found himself depressed and unhappy. He sent for his brother, a good-natured but rather an indifferent prince. The king said to him, "I am a great sinner; I fear to meet God." However, the prince only laughed at him. This did not help the king's disposition. Though he was a believer, the king had gotten a glimpse of his guilt for the way he'd been living lately, and he sincerely wanted help. In those days, it was customary that if the executioner sounded a trumpet on a man's door at any hour, it was a signal that he was to be led to his execution. The king sent the executioner in the dead of the night to sound the fateful blast at his brother's door. The prince realised with horror what was happening. Quickly dressing, he stepped to the door and was seized by the executioner, and dragged pale and trembling into the king's presence. In an agony of terror, he fell on his knees before his brother and begged to know how he had offended him. "My brother," answered the king, "if the sight of a human executioner is so terrible to you, shall not I, having grievously offended God, fear to be brought before the judgment seat of Christ?"

The fear of God will prevent you from selling out to the devil. What you will become has been predetermined but whether or not you will ever become it depends on you. Joseph's future was revealed to him while he was a teenager. It then took thirteen long years and a long winded route to get to the fulfilment of that destiny.

Had Joseph not feared God, the story could have been different, and the outcome could have been devastating for Joseph, his family and the entire people today referred to as the Hebrew nation. In the face of trials and tribulations, Joseph stood his ground and would not throw away the good upbringing and love legacy of his dad.

Joseph suffered for just over two years as a result of his refusal to enjoy a temporary pleasure with Potiphar's obsessed wife and compromise and sell his future because he feared God. He undoubtedly could have continued to enjoy free sex for some time which would have to come to an end one way or another, sooner than later. He would then have lost on every count and never become the leader that God intended him to become. You can read of this amazing true story in the book of Genesis from chapter 39 to 41. Let's read a bit of the story.

> *"Thus he left all that he had in Joseph's hand, and he did not know what he had except for the bread which he ate. Now Joseph was handsome in form and appearance. And it came to pass after these things that his master's wife cast longing eyes on Joseph, and she said, 'Lie with me.' But he refused and said to his master's wife, 'Look, my master does not know what is with me in the house, and he has committed all that he has to my hand. There is no one greater in this house than I, nor has he kept back anything from me but you, because you are his wife. How then can I do this great wickedness, and sin against God?'"* (Genesis 39:6-9).

That was all. Altogether, Joseph suffered for 13 years. However, he gave life and sustenance to millions of Egyptians and hundreds of thousands of Israelites until their final exit out of Egypt 430 years later. What a gain and what a trade!

Please let me end this chapter with these two scriptures,

> *"Don't be impressed with your own wisdom. Instead, fear the LORD and turn away from evil"* (Proverbs 3:7, NLT).

"One who is wise is cautious and turns away from evil, but a fool is reckless and careless" (Proverbs 14:16, ESV).

If only we know to what extent the effect of one act of disobedience will go, we will fear God. If only Adam, Abraham or David knew.

Chapter 2

If Adam Knew

The Dialogue

If Adam only knew that his disobedience would affect the whole world and how grievous the consequences would be, he probably would not have disobeyed God.

God asked Adam,

"... Where are you?"(Genesis 3:9).

That was not a quest for knowledge or education. God is omniscient; knowing all things. That also was not a question of physical location. God was only asking Adam so as to make him think of his spiritual position. Adam was spiritually lost. God had placed man in the highest of esteems, next only to Himself. In other words, man is subordinate only to God. This means we have been positioned higher than other heavenly beings, including angels.

"What is man that You take thought of him and the son of man that you care for him? Yet You have made

him a little lower than God, and You crown him with glory and majesty!" (Psalms 8:4-5, NASB).

I have used the NASB because it came closest to the original Hebrew word translated 'angels' in the KJV. The actual word is 'Elohiym' used 2604 times in the entire Bible as; God (2346x), god (244x), judge (5x), GOD (1x), goddess (2x), great (2x), mighty (2x), angels (1x) and exceeding (1x). The word is translated 'angels' only in the KJV of this passage. The error came from the Septuagint that replaced 'God' with 'angels'. Although, the translators got it wrong, this is how the KJV puts it.

"What is man, that thou art mindful of him, and the son of man, that thou visitest him? For thou hast made him a little lower than the angels, and hast crowned him with glory and honour" (Psalms 8:4-5, KJV).

God came to visit Adam "in the cool of the day" only to discover he was not in the spiritual position he was expected to be. Adam had left his privileged position of leadership, authority and dominion. He had allowed his worldly desire for power and equality (with God) to displace him from his position of rulership. His communion with God had been broken, and a spiritual gulf was created. Fear, loss of glory 'covering' and secrecy became part of human nature. The glory and majesty of God that covered Adam was uncovered, so he became naked, and because his innocence was stripped, he discovered his nakedness. Although Adam had been naked before the fall, he was not ashamed; he was innocent.

"And they were both naked, the man and his wife, and were not ashamed" (Genesis 2:25).

After the fall of the garden, men began to hide their true identity and nature from God and one another.

"He answered, 'I heard you in the garden, and I was afraid because I was naked; so I hid'" (Genesis 3:10, NIV).

Over 6,000 years (150 generations) later, we are still suffering the consequences. Most of these consequences are listed below derived from the curses in Genesis 3:17-19 and a few other passages in the Bible.

Consequences Of Adam's Fall

- It grieves the heart of God (Genesis 6:5-7).
- It brings guilt, anxiety and insecurity (Genesis 3:8; Psalms 51:3-4).
- It results in separation from God (Genesis 3:8; Psalms 51:3-4).
- It brings judgement and everlasting punishment (Matthew 25:46).
- It enslaves (Romans 6:17).
- It causes spiritual blindness (2 Corinthians 4:4).
- It causes spiritual death (Ephesians 2:1).
- It produces a lack of hope (Ephesians 2:12).
- It corrupts (Titus 1:5).
- It condemns (James 5:12).
- It brings shame and fear (Genesis 3:10).
- It causes pain (Genesis 3:16).

- It brings servitude (Genesis 3:16).

- It causes sorrow (Genesis 3:17).

- It brings curses (Genesis 3:17-18).

- It brings sweat and toil (Genesis 3:19).

- It causes physical death (Genesis 3:19).

- It produces suffering (Romans 8:22).

- It causes sickness (Romans 8:18; Micah 6:13).

This Is Too Much

I feel like jumping out of the pages of this book and screaming, "It is too much!" The consequences are too many for a little indulgence. It would be better to weigh the pleasure potentially derivable from disobedience against the immeasurable pain that must be endured by many. There are tens of thousands of diseases caused by the fall. For example, scientists currently estimate that over 10,000 of human diseases are known to be monogenic. Monogenic diseases result from modifications in a single gene occurring in all cells of the body. Though relatively rare, they affect millions of people worldwide. This is not to mention 10,000s of other diseases known to man.

Many people are still in disobedience to the word of God and Christians are taking the lead. We disobey God in too many ways to count. We abuse His grace in the belief that 'morning by morning, His mercies' we would see continually. The Lord is asking us to avoid sin and disobedience rather than seek mercy all the time.

Sin Is Attractive

I read about a family that visited the Niagara Falls several years ago. The season was spring, and the family noticed ice was flowing down the river. There they saw large blocks of ice rushing toward the falls and also discovered that carcasses of dead fish were embedded in the ice. Scores of Seagulls came riding down the river to feed on the dead fishes. Close to the time the ice would approach the edge of the fall, the Seagulls would stretch out their wings to fly and escape from falling.

There was, however one seagull that seemed to delay and the family wondered when it would leave. It was engrossed in the carcass of a fish, and when it finally came to the brink of the falls, out went its powerful wings. The bird flapped and flapped and even lifted the ice out of the water, and it was assumed it would soon escape. However, it had delayed too long so that its claws had frozen into the ice. The weight of the ice was too great, and the Seagull plunged into the abyss.

Sin is attractive, but it can also ensnare. It is easier to avoid its lure than to quit its grip. There is nothing the enemy will offer without compromise. It is usually harder to give up material possessions of this world or the pleasures of life once it has been tasted. Sins will take us to our destruction if we become too attached to them.

Let Me Repeat

Had Adam known what we now know, he probably would have given more thought to his action. We know that what we do or omit to do knowing we are supposed to do might end up affecting four generations after us. Such knowledge was not available to Adam. The summary is this: The entire universe is suffering the consequences of Adam's wrong choices.

> "For we know that the whole creation groans and labours with birth pangs together until now" (Romans 8:22).

The question that must now be answered is this: What would it take to reverse this catastrophe? The answer is found in Romans 8:19. We need to come out of hiding. We need to show up, step up and stand up. We manifest His power when we stop hiding and begin to establish God's kingdom here on earth.

> "For the earnest expectation of the creature waiteth for the manifestation of the sons of God" (Romans 8:19, KJV).

Chapter 3

IF ABRAHAM KNEW

The Dialogue

While the sin of disobedience committed by Adam affected and still affects the whole world, another man's sin affected an entire nation. A disobedience may not affect the while world but it may affect a family. If Abraham only knew that his affair with Hagar would cause, to this day, an unending enmity between her seed and that of Sarah, he probably would not have had it. Let us look at some of the consequences of Abraham's compromise.

First of all, Abram suffered thirteen years of separation and silence from God. According to the Bible, between 86 and 99 years of his life, heaven was silent.

> *"And Abram was eighty-six years old when Hagar bore him Ishmael. When Abram was ninety-nine years old, the LORD appeared to him and said, 'I AM God Almighty; walk before Me and be blameless'"* *(Genesis 16:16-17:1, NIV).*

Each time Abram would kneel to pray, he would encounter a dead silence. Heaven was a brass. God refused to speak to Abram haven demonstrated his inability to handle his family by allowing the society to influence him to the extent that he sinned against God.

Perhaps heaven is closed over your life because you have not kept to the previous instruction and agreement you had with God.

Secondly, Sarai was tormented and despised by her maid. What rights had a slave girl to treat her mistress in such a way, someone who gave her an undeserved privilege? Would it have been better for Sarai to remain childless than to be despised and humiliated by someone she called a servant?

Thinking about it, Sarai was only observing what was culturally acceptable. She was not looking for a mistress or someone with whom to share her marital home. No sensible woman would do that. It is amazing how what initially appeared innocent suddenly turned chaotic. It must have been difficult for Sarai to imagine her husband sharing his time with another woman, let alone her maid.

Hagar abused her privileges. She was excused from many slave duties so she could be physically, emotionally and sexually ready for Abram during the night hours. She was beginning to enjoy freedom and was gradually becoming emotionally attached to Abram. She started to dream of the possibility of permanently living in the palace as the only and rightful mother of the promised child. She thought for a moment of the possibility of Sarai remaining permanently childless. Of course, she could not show her feelings or share them with anyone. She could not even offend Madam Sarai. If she did, she could be quickly replaced by a more eligible alternative. She had to keep quiet 'until such a time.'

Then her moment came, the pregnancy test arrived positive. She had the scarce commodity. She may not be a valued slave, but she suddenly became an invaluable mother-to-be. She was able to give Abram what Sarai her mistress could not. For a moment, she thought, 'I am better than Sarai.' So she began to threaten abortion if Sarai did not cooperate or behave herself. Her privileged position got to her head, and Sarai was despised.

Sarai now wished she had been a little more patient. What is she now to do? She blamed everything on her husband for encouraging his desire and desperation for a son to affect him without giving thought to the consequence his action would have on her. She expected him to step in and protect her from being despised by her slave. When he did not, she became angry with him and picked a fight. Abram would not have that also. So he gave Sarai the responsibility to mete out any punishment deemed appropriate to her maid. The situation became so bad they could not be bothered about having a son anymore. Not with that kind of attitude from a slave anyway.

What Was Their Wrong?

Why should they suffer? What was their wrong? Such are the questions billions of people are asking without any hope of receiving any relevant answers. On our streets and in the pews are many people suffering for the sins of few, particularly those close to them. Majority do not know they are paying for something they did not purchase. They do not know why they have been singled out, or what could be done to get them out. What a tragedy?

What Was Her Wrong?

Hagar was a slave girl minding her business when she received summon. She would begin to wonder what wrong she had committed. Why was her mistress suddenly taking interest in her, amongst comparable options? Was any one of the slaves expecting such privilege, knowing the culture? When the time comes, who would be the favoured one? Did any of the slave girls do anything to get noticed knowing the likelihood of this happening – work harder maybe or dress more neatly? What was the reason Hagar was chosen? No one knows.

Hagar could not say 'No' even if she were not interested in the proposal. This too was a possibility. Knowing that Sarai was only interested in herself, Hagar could have been uninterested in the idea of using her as the mother of Sarah's adopted child. She could have felt violated, yet she could not refuse the offer. Otherwise, she could have been killed, sold or thrown out of the palace. Who knows what could have happened to a disobedient slave? So Hagar put her life in the hands of her master and mistress knowing she could never replace Sarai in Abram's heart or become the first wife though she were the first mother. She knew when push comes to shove; she would be the one to leave. As thought, it did, but she still had to comply.

Hagar reluctantly offered her body but not her soul. She would bear a child for Sarai but not without some form of reward. From now on, she would not wash plates or do the bedrooms. She would not do the laundry or mop the floor. She is now a wife. She would no longer submit to her mistress. So Sarai felt despised when Hagar refused to do the slave chores. Hagar was tormented and had misery as a result. However, she was not driven from home. When she could no longer endure the hardship, Hagar fled for her life; from misery and affliction.

> "...Then Sarai mistreated Hagar; so she fled away. The Angel of the LORD said to her, "Return to your mistress, and submit yourself under her hand." The angel of the LORD also said to her: 'You are now with child and you will have a son. You shall call his name Ishmael, for the LORD has heard of your misery'" (Genesis 16:6, 9, 11, NIV).

Hagar then received a warning by the angel she encountered. So she went back home to her mistress in the hope God was going to sort things out. However, things got worse. Later we read of a 26-year old man enjoying the pleasure in tormenting his 12-year old sibling. Imagine a young boy being tormented by a brother more than twice his age for sins he did not commit. This was no token sibling rivalry; it was torment of the highest degree. It was so bad God's attention was required, and excommunication was the given verdict. On this occasion, Hagar was thrown out with her son.

> "The child grew and was weaned, and on the day Isaac was weaned Abraham held a great feast. But Sarah saw that the son whom Hagar the Egyptian had borne to Abraham was mocking, and she said to Abraham, 'Get rid of that slave woman and her son, for that slave woman's son will never share in the inheritance with my son Isaac.' The matter displeased Abraham greatly because it concerned his son. But God said to him, 'Do not be so distressed about the boy and your

maidservant. Listen to whatever Sarah tells you, because it is through Isaac that your offspring will be reckoned. I will make the son of the maidservant into a nation also, because he is your offspring. Early the next morning Abraham took some food and a skin of water and gave them to Hagar. He set them on her shoulders and then sent her off with the boy. She went on her way and wandered in the desert of Beersheba" (Genesis 21:8-14, NIV).

The two halves of 26 years must have been tormenting for Hagar. During the first 13 years, Hagar lived the life of a wife valued only for her body and the next 13 years, fighting for the rights of her innocent son. She got battered from all angles by her mistress.

What About Ishmael?

Though he scoffed at his brother, he was himself a victim of the situation. He did not choose to be born to a family struggling to keep their heads up in a society that says your family is not complete unless you buy, beg or steal a child, adopt or give birth to one. They lived in a society that valued women not for their worth, but for their ability to conceive and birth choice children at their desired time; an insane society similar to what exists even in the 21st Century.

Come to think of it, who would blame Ishmael? He grew up in his first 13 years thinking and living the life of a promised seed in the palace of Abraham. He had the entire wealth of his father to himself. His father cherished and nourished him as his only son to the point that he was even displeased with the thought of him leaving home. He might not have been a child of choice, but he was a child to choose nonetheless. Perhaps he even knew he was not the promised child yet he grew up as the only one. Beside him there was no other. Even 13 years after his birth, Sarai still could not conceive, and so the hope of the choice child was gone.

The second positive pregnancy test in the life of Abraham occurred before his death. Nine months later, Isaac was miraculously born when Ishmael was in his second teenage year – 14 years old. All hopes disappeared. Hopes of being the heir apparent; the right to the palace and the right of the firstborn were in a moment lost. For the next 12 years, things were never going to be the same. As Isaac started growing up, Ishmael began to realise his special privileges would soon begin to diminish and eventually taken away. What could he have done? So he began to scoff.

We have seen that Abraham's sin was not only punished on Abraham but his entire family. Sarah was despised, and so were Isaac, Ishmael and Hagar.

The Whole World Groans

"The Scriptures say that Abraham had two sons, one from his slave-wife and one from his freeborn wife. The son of the slave-wife was born in a human attempt to bring about the fulfilment of God's promise. But the son of the freeborn wife was born as God's own fulfilment of His promise. Now these two women serve as an illustration of God's two covenants. Hagar, the slave-wife, represents Mount Sinai where people first became enslaved to the law. And now Jerusalem is just like Mount Sinai in Arabia, because

she and her children live in slavery. But Sarah, the free woman, represents the heavenly Jerusalem. And she is our mother. That is what Isaiah meant when he prophesied, 'Rejoice, O childless woman! Break forth into loud and joyful song, even though you never gave birth to a child. For the woman who could bear no children now has more than all the other women.' And you dear brothers and sisters are children of the promise, just like Isaac. And we who are born of the Holy Spirit are persecuted by those who want us to keep by Ishmael, the son of the slave-wife. But what do the Scriptures say about that? 'Get rid of the slave and her son, for the son of the slave woman will not share the family inheritance with the free woman's son.' So, dear brothers and sisters, we are not children of the slave woman, obligated to the law. We are children of the free woman, acceptable to God because of our faith" (Galatians 4:21-31, NLT).

The summary of the scripture above is this. The problem in the Middle East today is because of the human attempt to bring about the fulfilment of God's promise. Paul hit the nail on the head. It cannot be simpler than that.

We sometimes think of how to help God. Since He lives in heaven, we think He probably does not understand our pains and frustrations. God does not need our help to fulfil His promises. He is sovereign, omnipotent and all-sufficient. We end up complicating our situations and mess up when we try to help God. After Abraham had attempted to help God, he received a stark warning.

"...I AM God Almighty; walk before Me and be blameless" (Genesis 17:1, NIV).

Part of the cure for sin is obedience. However, obedience alone is not enough. The permanent cure for sin includes walking before God. We sometimes walk with God. After that, we follow God. We need to progress to walking before God. When we do, He can keep us under His watchful eyes. Not that He cannot see us wherever we may be, but we need to place ourselves under His scrutiny. We do this by finding out what displeases Him through reading His word and keeping it at the centre of our hearts.

"How can a young person stay pure? By obeying Your word and following its rules. I have tried my best to find you – don't let me wander from your commands. I have hidden Your word in my heart, that I might not sin against You" (Psalms 119:9-11, NLT).

We stay away from sin by the observance of the word of God but prevent going into sin by finding out what God says about it in the first place. Abraham did not stay away from sin, and as a result, the lives of many innocent souls were affected.

You may be suffering the consequence of things you knew nothing about; may be of parents or guardians; may be from governing authorities of your country; there is hope for you. You can be set free. You do not have to live with it for the rest of your life. Ask God to forgive your ancestors where the offences are known and ask Him to set you free. Where restitution is appropriate and affordable, you may need to do so. This must be done with the utmost sensitivity. If you feel overwhelmed by the burden, share it with your spiritual leader and God will grant unto you liberty and freedom.

Chapter 4

IF DAVID KNEW

Adam's disobedience affected the whole world, and Abraham's impatience affected the Hebrew race primarily, but for David, his family would feel the consequences of his sin.

In the Book of Esther, one night with the king brought deliverance to the Jewish nation. However, in the Book of 2 Samuel, one night with the king brought a curse on a family. David's one night with Bathsheba had dire consequences. It costs his family dearly. You can read the entire story in 2 Samuel 11 and 12.

First it resulted in the death of an innocent warrior, Uriah, Bathsheba's husband.

> *"In the morning it happened that David wrote a letter to Joab and sent it by the hand of Uriah. And he wrote in the letter, saying, 'Set Uriah in the forefront of the hottest battle, and retreat from him, that he may be struck down and die.' So it was, while Joab besieged the city, that he assigned Uriah to a place where he knew there were valiant men. Then the men of the city came out and fought with Joab. And some of the people*

of the servants of David fell; and Uriah the Hittite died also" (2 Samuel 11:14-17).

Secondly, it resulted in the death of an innocent baby David fathered out of adultery.

"When David saw that his servants were whispering, David perceived that the child was dead. Therefore, David said to his servants, 'Is the child dead?' And they said, 'He is dead'" (2 Samuel 12:19).

Thirdly, there was a curse placed on the family. From then on, the family was going to be perpetually attacked, and there were going to be constant battles within and without. They were to be fighting each other within and warring and warding away enemies without.

"'Now therefore, the sword shall never depart from your house, because you have despised Me, and have taken the wife of Uriah the Hittite to be your wife.' Thus says the LORD: 'Behold, I will raise up adversity against you from your own house; and I will take your wives before your eyes and give them to your neighbour, and he shall lie with your wives in the sight of this sun. 'For you did it secretly, but I will do this thing before all Israel, before the sun'" (2 Samuel 12:10-12).

There were also going to be humiliation and disgrace by David's son. The dynasty was going to be dishonoured, and royalty besmirched. As was foretold by the prophet Nathan, Absalom publicly slept with David's concubines.

"And Ahithophel said to Absalom, 'Go in to your father's concubines, whom he has left to keep the house; and all Israel will hear that you are abhorred by your father. Then the hands of all who are with you will be strong.' So they pitched a tent for Absalom on the top of the house, and Absalom went in to his father's concubines in the sight of all Israel. Now the advice of Ahithophel, which he gave in those days, was as if one had inquired at the oracle of God. So was all the advice of Ahithophel both with David and with Absalom" (2 Samuel 16:21-23).

The penalty for any offence in many cases always outweighs the temporary pleasures that may have been derived from it. Also, the punishment usually outlives the offender and many innocent generations after may be infected or affected or both. We should allow the Spirit of God to illuminate our hearts and reveal to us the dangers of our ungodly and immoral actions irrespective of what the world around us believes.

So how can you prevent all these calamities and protect your future? I will discuss this in the next chapter.

Chapter 5

HIS TACTICS ARE STILL THE SAME

He Lurks In The Dark

Derek Curtis Bok, a lawyer, educator and the former president of Harvard University once said this: "If you think education is expensive, try ignorance." He was right. Ignorance can be more expensive than education. It is wrong to say that what you do not know cannot hurt you. It can. If you are unaware of your rights as a child of God, the devil will take advantage of you.

> *"Lest Satan should take advantage of us; for we are not ignorant of his devices" (2 Corinthians 2:11).*

It is the devil's deliberate act to keep Christians ignorant. Ignorance is his greatest and most potent weapon. He would do all that is in his power to make and keep people ignorant. He keeps people in the dark and blinds the eyes of the seekers.

> *"Whose minds the god of this age has blinded, who do not believe, lest the light of the gospel of the glory of*

Christ, who is the image of God, should shine on them" (2 Corinthians 4:4).

The devil lurks and lives in the dark. He lies in wait, skulks, prowls, loiters, hangs about and creeps around in the dark recesses of our life. No wonder most evils are done in the dark. Do not be fooled when the devil appear as your helper and pretend to be the angel of light. He is still the prince of this dark world.

"And no wonder! For Satan himself transforms himself into an angel of light" (2 Corinthians 11:14).

He Is Deceptive

The devil is a deceiver. His other classic vice is deception. That is why he is called the "father of lies." Lying or deception is his second nature. This guy is crafty.

"But I fear, lest somehow, as the serpent deceived Eve by his craftiness, so your minds may be corrupted from the simplicity that is in Christ" (2 Corinthians 11:3).

"For Adam was formed first, then Eve. And Adam was not deceived, but the woman being deceived, fell into transgression" (1 Timothy 2:13-14).

Paul said Adam was not deceived. No, he could not be deceived. Adam was not deceived because he could not be deceived. Deception can only happen where the "truth" is not known or not fully understood. It will take much effort for someone to be persuaded that the green apple he or she is holding is actually a red apple unless he or she does not understand colours very well. Where the devil senses the smallest degree of uncertainty, he would then plant doubt. He made Eve doubt God's instruction because he measured her depth of comprehension of the command not to eat of the fruit of the tree in the midst of the garden and perhaps found it was flawed.

> *"Now the serpent was MORE CUNNING than any beast of the field which the LORD God had made. And he said to the woman, "Has God INDEED said, 'You shall not eat of every tree of the garden'?" (Genesis 3:1).*

It was a lot easier to deceive Eve. She either did not fully grasp what the command was or did not realise the gravity of the offence. The command not to eat of the fruit of the tree in the midst of the garden was not directly given to her. It must have been relayed to her by Adam.

So Satan went for Eve and deliberately avoided any confrontation with Adam. The devil knew Adam would have told him straight away what God's instruction was. When Adam ate the forbidden fruit, his action was not in any way of an omission. Rather, it was an act of disobedience.

Paradoxically, it may still be possible for someone to sin even with the knowledge of the truth. This happens when someone ignores the consequences of his or her action. This is not usually a result of deception, but it is based on the promise of a higher reward for the disobedience; in this case, the promised of attaining god-ship.

The devil still promises people all sorts today – fame, fortune and fantasies. You could be his next target.

He Is A Master Planner

The devil is a strategist par excellence. He is a schemer and a thinker. He plans, plots and executes those plans to a fault. He does not like to hit and miss. Although he is an opportunist, he can wait for as long as it would take before launching an attack. Take a look at this;

> *"Lest Satan should take advantage of us; for we are not ignorant of his devices" (2 Corinthians 2:11).*

The word 'devices' is the Greek word 'noēma.' Other translations used the word thoughts, schemes and designs. The word occurs six times in the New Testament. Four times 'noēma' was translated as 'minds', once as 'devices' and once as 'thoughts.' For a better understanding of the word, I will list the other five scriptures.

> *"But their minds were blinded. For until this day the same veil remains unlifted in the reading of the Old Testament, because the veil is taken away in Christ" (2 Corinthians 3:14).*

> *"Whose minds the god of this age has blinded, who do not believe, lest the light of the gospel of the glory of Christ, who is the image of God, should shine on them" (2 Corinthians 4:4).*

> *"But I fear, lest somehow, as the serpent deceived Eve by his craftiness, so your minds may be corrupted from the simplicity that is in Christ" (2 Corinthians 11:3).*

"And the peace of God, which surpasses all understanding, will guard your hearts and minds through Christ Jesus" (Philippians 4:7).

"Casting down arguments and every high thing that exalts itself against the knowledge of God, bringing every thought into captivity to the obedience of Christ" (2 Corinthians 10:5).

Did you notice that all but one of the six scriptures spoke with respect to spiritual warfare, focusing on thoughts and minds? Satan's schemes are his thoughts and minds. This is why I said he is a strategist par excellence. To defeat the devil, we would then need to think on a higher dimension. We cannot think like him; we have to think like Christ. The battlefield is our minds. That is where we can be defeated or exalted.

We would not allow the devil to infiltrate us with junk. We would not buy his suggestions and lies. We would focus our minds on things that are above which are eternal and not on things beneath which are temporal. We would let our minds follow after God and things that are godly. We cannot and will not be defeated by the devil. We are smarter than he is. We are of God. We would cast down arguments and every high thing that exalts itself against the knowledge of God. We operate on a higher dimension. We would beat the strategist par excellence at his own game. We are not fighting like ones beating the air. We would prevail, not in our strength, but through Him who strengthen us. Where we have failed, we would look back and launch higher. We are overcomers and more than conquerors. Amen.

Other Scriptures About Ignorance

"For I do not desire, brethren, that you should be ignorant of this mystery, lest you should be wise in your own opinion, that blindness in part has happened to Israel until the fullness of the Gentiles has come in" (Romans 11:25).

"Now concerning spiritual gifts, brethren, I do not want you to be ignorant:" (1 Corinthians 12:1).

"Having their understanding darkened, being alienated from the life of God, because of the ignorance that is in them, because of the blindness of their heart;" (Ephesians 4:18).

Chapter 6

ONE, TWO, THREE, NO

One: The Lust of the Eyes. Two: The Lust of the Flesh. Three: The Pride of Life. After that, NO.

Satan has an agenda. His aim is to push his agenda until his targets succumb. In the last chapter, we saw who Satan is but we would now see how he operates in the life of the believer. The scripture below sums up the devil's old tricks. If you can say 'NO' to him in these three areas, you will never again be conquered. That is why I titled this chapter, "One, Two, Three, 'NO.'" Here it goes;

> *"Do not love the world or the things in the world. If anyone loves the world, the love of the Father is not in him. For all that is in the world – THE LUST OF THE FLESH, THE LUST OF THE EYES, AND THE PRIDE OF LIFE – is not of the Father but is of the world. And the world is passing away, and the lust of it; but he who does the will of God abides forever" (1 John 2:15-17, Emphasis Mine).*

The Lust Of The Flesh

The lust of the flesh is simply the cravings or desires of the body. Our bodies have need for food, drink, touch, intimacy, healing, and more. Although these are general necessities of life, they can also become problems in that we can fall prey of its lusting. Lusting is craving for the forbidden rather than the allowed. Love is a wholesome desire, whereas lust is a perverted one. Lust seeks after fornication or adultery, gluttony, alternate medicine, etc. Basically, body needs and desires met through the wrong channels constitute lust. When we succumb to the demands of the flesh, we make the devil the winner.

Thomas Costain's history, The Three Edwards, described the life of Raynald III, a fourteenth-century duke in what is now Belgium. Grossly overweight, Raynald was commonly called by his Latin nickname, Crassus, which means "fat."

After a violent quarrel, Raynald's younger brother Edward led a successful revolt against him. Edward captured Raynald but did not kill him. Instead, he built a room around Raynald in the Nieuwkerk castle and promised him he could regain his title and property as soon as he was able to leave the room.

This would not have been difficult for most people since the room had several windows and a door of near-normal size, and none was locked or barred. The problem was Raynald's size. To regain his freedom, he needed to lose weight. However, Edward knew his older brother, and each day he sent a variety of delicious foods. Instead of dieting his way out of prison, Raynald grew fatter.

When Duke Edward was accused of cruelty, he had a ready answer: "My brother is not a prisoner. He may leave when he so wills." Raynald stayed in that room for ten years and wasn't released until after Edward died in battle. By then his health was so ruined he died within a year. Raynald was a prisoner of his own appetite.

A genuinely redeemed child of God does not yield to the dictates of the flesh. This is not saying that he or she might not be tempted, just that he masters his desires and would not allow the body to dominate or rule. We have the power to refuse the devil's suggestions to lust. To claim to be in the spirit and yet yield to the demands of the flesh is a contradiction in terms.

> *"I say then: Walk in the Spirit, and you shall not fulfill the lust of the flesh. For the flesh lusts against the Spirit, and the Spirit against the flesh; and these are contrary to one another, so that you do not do the things that you wish. But if you are led by the Spirit, you are not under the law"* (Galatians 5:16-18).

The Lust Of The Eyes

The devil uses a similar method when it comes to the eyes. We appreciate the wonders of God's creation and behold with awe the beauty of His love through the things we observe with our eyes. The tool God gave can be used for bad cause when we permit the devil its control. The God-given ability for vision is a good thing that can be used in love and to further a good cause. The same in Satan's hand can become a lust tool. He is well aware of damages he can exert using our eyes against us. Just take a look at the media; the internet, the television, the papers, the lights at the casinos and the ornate presentations in the windows. Why do you think nudity is being normalised? Sex sells for a reason. We are being drawn to many lustful things in the things we see.

The Pride Of Life

Let's face it; we all take pride in our achievements and possessions. We show off with the certificates on our walls both at home and in our offices. Some list the titles after their names and others, before their names. Our business cards, our cell phones and our cars are today's status symbols. We pride ourselves in the knowledge we possess and our educational achievements. Coated in immodesty, vanity, self-importance, smugness, conceit, egotism, vanity, arrogance and feelings of superiority, pride destroys. It is the temptation to want to be our own boss, the need to be in charge of our lives. It is the temptation to want to be valued and be self-sufficient leading to pride and boasting.

These are the things – the lust of the flesh, the lust of the eyes and the pride of life – that comes between us and God. They may be three, but just one is strong enough to derail us and put us at odds with God, and the devil does not have to use the three before we become enemies of our creator. However, in most cases, the enemy of your soul will combine the three assaults to secure your capture. He did it to Eve, Potiphar's wife, Achan, David, but could not succeed with our Lord Jesus.

Chapter 7

WE'VE SEEN THIS BEFORE

Satan is predictable. He doesn't have new tricks. He is not innovative, and neither is he creative. All he does is to remodel and repackage himself. From the day time began and until now, he is still using the same old tricks. Shouldn't we have known; shouldn't we have learnt?

The scripture below sums up the devil's old tricks;

> "Do not love the world or the things in the world. If anyone loves the world, the love of the Father is not in him. For all that is in the world – the lust of the flesh, the lust of the eyes, and the pride of life – is not of the Father but is of the world. And the world is passing away, and the lust of it; but he who does the will of God abides forever" (1 John 2:15-17).

Whatever we strongly desire can become the route to our downfall. Desires are not in themselves wrong but Satan can capitalise on the strong desires, and it then becomes desperation. Desperation may then lead to compromise. This then becomes a weakness of the flesh and turns to become a stronghold. However, if you are aware of the devil's tricks, you can gain an understanding of the ways to prevent the desire to be taken advantage of.

As I hope to show from Bible passages, the New Covenant believers have an advantage the Old Covenant believers did not. We can see the devil at work. Come with me, and I will show you what the Bible say about this adversary.

The following people were tempted the same way, and I think their temptations teach us a great deal about the schemes of the devil seen in the previous chapter. It follows a pattern; the lust of the eyes (the sight), the lust of the flesh (the desire), and the pride of life (the pursuit).

Eve's Temptation

Adam and Eve were given the rare privilege of feeding on the lush provided in the Garden of Eden. There was however a tree of which they were forbidden to eat of its fruit. That was the one right in the middle of the garden – the tree of the knowledge of good and evil. Remember, I said earlier that Eve did not receive the instruction directly from God; her husband told her of God's wish. This gave Satan the opportunity to strike. So he went to the woman. Read with me how she responded to the Devil's proposition.

> "When the woman saw that the fruit of the tree was good for food and pleasing to the eye, and also desirable for gaining wisdom, she took some and ate it. She also gave some to her husband, who was with her, and he ate it" (Genesis 3:6 NIV).

"The woman was convinced. She saw that the tree was beautiful and its fruit looked delicious, and she wanted the wisdom it would give her. So she took some of the fruit and ate it. Then she gave some to her husband, who was with her, and he ate it, too" (Genesis 3:6 NLT).

Sight, desire and pursuit are going to be the pattern used by the devil, both in this instance and those that will follow until the end of time.

- Sight – "She saw that the tree was beautiful, and its fruit looked delicious," (NLT)

- Desire – "and also desirable for gaining wisdom," (NIV)

- Pursuit – "she took some and ate it." (NIV)

Lot's Temptation

Contrary to God's express instruction (Genesis Chapter 12), Abram took Lot his nephew with him on a journey to a strange land. Both their businesses grew and were too big for the location south of Bethel. So their herdsmen began to fight for resources to take care of their growing flock. This led to the squabble between Abram and his nephew. Being the older, Abram yielded his ground and offered Lot the opportunity to be the first to choose from the vast land that surrounded them. Let us follow from Lot's response.

Lot took a long look at the fertile plains of the Jordan Valley in the direction of Zoar. The whole area was well watered everywhere, like the garden of the LORD or the beautiful land of Egypt. (This was before the LORD destroyed Sodom and Gomorrah.) Lot chose for himself the whole Jordan Valley to the east of them. He went there with his flocks and servants and parted company with his uncle Abram" (Genesis 13:10-11 NLT).

> *"Lot looked. He saw the whole plain of the Jordan spread out, well-watered (this was before God destroyed Sodom and Gomorrah), like God's garden, like Egypt, and stretching all the way to Zoar. Lot took the whole plain of the Jordan. Lot set out to the east" (Genesis 13:10-11, MSG).*

Did you see the pattern again in this discourse; the sight, desire and pursuit?

- Sight – "Lot took a long look at the fertile plains ..." (NLT)

- Desire – "whole area was well watered everywhere, like the garden of the LORD or the beautiful land of Egypt." (NLT)

- Pursuit – "Lot took the whole plain of the Jordan." (MSG)

Mrs. Potiphar's Temptation

Joseph was sold into slavery by his brothers because they could not handle the discovery that he was going to become their future leader being the eleventh son of Jacob. Arriving Egypt, he found himself serving under Pharaoh's Captain-of-the-Guard, named Potiphar. There was an exchange between Joseph and Mrs. Potiphar. This is where we pick the story up.

Contrary to many teachings regarding Joseph being tempted, it is nowhere recorded that he entertained any desire for Mrs. Potiphar in his brief spell at her residence. The story was about Potiphar's wife, not about Joseph. She was the one who had a crush on Joseph. The story is found in Genesis 39:6-12.

> *"Thus he left all that he had in Joseph's hand, and he did not know what he had except for the bread which he ate. Now Joseph was handsome in form and appearance. And it came to pass after these things that his master's wife cast longing eyes on Joseph, and she said, "Lie with me." But he refused and said to his master's wife, "Look, my master does not know what is with me in the house, and he has committed all that he has to my hand. There is no one greater in this house than I, nor has he kept back anything from me but you, because you are his wife. How then can I do this great wickedness, and sin against God?" So it was, as she spoke to Joseph day by day, that he did not heed her, to lie with her or to be with her. But it happened about this time, when Joseph went into the house to do his work, and none of the men of the house was inside, that she caught him by his garment, saying, "Lie with me." But he left his garment in her hand, and fled and ran outside" (Genesis 39:6-12).*

Although Joseph was 'handsome in form and appearance,' 'he refused' Mrs. Potiphar's hit on him, gave a reason for his refusal, considered yielding as a 'great wickedness, and sin against God,' and fled when harassed. This does not look like someone who was tempted. Though he was raised in a polygamous environment, he had the fear of God and had conquered 'youthful lust.'

Let us now look at the reasons I concluded that it was Mrs. Potiphar's that was tempted. It fitted perfectly into the same pattern we have seen so far.

- Sight – "… his master's (Potiphar's) wife cast longing eyes on Joseph,"

- Desire – "… and she said, 'Lie with me.'" And "… she spoke to Joseph day by day,"

- Pursuit – "… she caught him by his garment,"

Achan's Temptation

The setting is the lost battle of Ai. The Children of Israel conquered Jericho, but someone took what was set apart for the Lord. Achan was exposed as the perpetrator. Here is his explanation.

> *"When I saw among the spoils a beautiful Babylonian garment, two hundred shekels of silver, and a wedge of gold weighing fifty shekels, I coveted them and took them. And there they are, hidden in the earth in the midst of my tent, with the silver under it"* (Joshua 7:21).

Achan's temptation was not going to be different from our pattern of sight, desire and pursuit. We have seen this before. Amazing isn't it?

- Sight – "When I saw among the spoils a beautiful Babylonian garment, two hundred shekels of silver, and a wedge of gold weighing fifty shekels,"

- Desire – "I coveted them ..."

- Pursuit – "... and took them."

David's Temptation

"In the spring, at the time when kings go off to war, David sent Joab out with the king's men and the whole Israelite army. They destroyed the Ammonites and besieged Rabbah. But David remained in Jerusalem" (2 Samuel 11:1, NIV).

That was the setting – a king refusing to go to war when he was supposed to. See what happened next.

"Late one afternoon, after his midday rest, David got out of bed and was walking on the roof of the palace. As he looked out over the city, he noticed a woman of unusual beauty taking a bath. He sent someone to find out who she was, and he was told, "She is Bathsheba, the daughter of Eliam and the wife of Uriah the Hittite. Then David sent messengers to get her; and when she came to the palace, he slept with her. She had just completed the purification rites after having her menstrual period. Then she returned home" (2 Samuel 11:2-4, NLT).

- Sight – "As he looked out over the city, he noticed a woman of unusual beauty taking a bath."

- Desire – "He sent someone to find out who she was, and he was told,"

- Pursuit – "Then David sent messengers to get her; and when she came to the palace, he slept with her."

What a fall? It's the same pattern, again.

Child of God, Satan has not got any new strategy except to disguise the same one he is used to all these years. Watch what you see, it may turn to a strong desire that may then cause you to fall. The lust of the eyes, the lust of the flesh and the pride of life are the only ways Satan can get you. James put it succinctly in James 1:13-15,

> "Let no one say when he is tempted, "I am tempted by God"; for God cannot be tempted by evil, nor does He Himself tempt anyone. But each one is tempted when he is drawn away by his own desires and enticed. Then, when desire has conceived, it gives birth to sin; and sin, when it is full-grown, brings forth death" (James 1:13-15).

What about Jesus?

The devil is no respecter of persons. He went for the big boss. Our Lord Jesus Christ was not exempt from attacks. You would however have thought Satan would use a different tactic when he came to Jesus, but you see, it is not in him to innovate. In order to destroy God's plan for man's redemption, what Satan tried and succeeded with Eve, Lot, Mrs. Potiphar, Achan, and David, were to be tried on Jesus.

Jesus' Temptation

"Then Jesus was led up by the Spirit into the wilderness to be tempted by the devil. And when He had fasted forty days and forty nights, afterward He was hungry" (Matthew 4:1-2).

This is the background to the whole story. After fasting forty days and forty nights, it was natural for Jesus to feel hungry. That was the desire Satan needed to see so he can take advantage of Jesus. Remember, it was through food that Adam lost. It just happened that the devil's defeat was to come through food. Fortunately, what the first Adam could not resist, the second Adam could not consent. Let's read on.

Jesus Repressed His Desire (Hunger)

Although Jesus was hungry, dining with the devil was not an option. Jesus had to repress His hunger. You do not have to eat just anything because you are hungry. So many people have dipped their hands into the same plate the devil is eating from and they are direly paying for it. Several of our failings may be avoided if only we can defer our want to another time.

"Now when the tempter came to Him, he said, "If You are the Son of God, command that these stones become bread." But He answered and said, "It is written, 'Man shall not live by bread alone, but by every word that proceeds from the mouth of God'" (Matthew 4:3-4).

Jesus Rebuffs The Pursuit (Glory)

Knowing who you are is essential to not yielding to what others suggest you should be. A healthy self-image will help you to not want to prove your worth. When the devil suggested to Jesus to jump, there was no need to question what the reactions of the angels would have been. They would show up. However, Jesus would have lost the battle to the devil because He would from then on be subject to him.

> *"Then the devil took Him up into the holy city, set Him on the pinnacle of the temple, and said to Him, "If You are the Son of God, throw Yourself down. For it is written: 'He shall give His angels charge over you,' and, 'In their hands they shall bear you up, lest you dash your foot against a stone.'" Jesus said to him, "It is written again, 'You shall not tempt the LORD your God'" (Matthew 4:5-7).*

Jesus Refused The Sight (Look)

Seen so far, most temptations started with sighting a desirable object or person. In the encounter with Jesus, the Master declined when Satan showed Him all the kingdoms of the world.

> *"Again, the devil took Him up on an exceedingly high mountain, and showed Him all the kingdoms of the world and their glory. And he said to Him, "All these things I will give You if You will fall down and worship me." Then Jesus said to him, "Away with you, Satan! For it is written, 'You shall worship the LORD your God, and Him only you shall*

serve.' "Then the devil left Him, and behold, angels came and ministered to Him" (Matthew 4:8-11).

Chapter 8

HOW TO PROTECT YOUR SPIRIT

Recognise And Identify The Areas Of Weaknesses

It is dangerous not to be aware of the areas you are weak. I am surprised when people say they do not know their areas of weaknesses. Do you know yours? Let's find out.

Have you ever committed fornication or adultery before? Have you ever lied or sworn falsely in all your life? Have you ever been drunk or over-eaten before? Have you ever taken what was not yours or ever coveted your friend's goods before? If the answer to any of them is 'No', take a look at the following.

The list goes like this: wickedness, malice; envy, murder, strife, deception, evil-mindedness, backbiting, hating God, violence, pride, boasting, inventing of evil things, disobeying parents.

If you have ever done any of these things more than once and have never effectively dealt with it, this may be your area of weakness. It is very likely the devil will continue to tempt you in those areas until they are adequately dealt with.

There is another concern I would like to explore. There are people who know the areas of their weaknesses, but deny the ability of the devil to tempt them in those areas. This can be seen as pride or arrogance. No one is ever too big or too spiritual to be tempted of the devil. The devil tempted our Lord and Saviour Jesus, and he is not a respecter of persons.

> *"Therefore let him who thinks he stands take heed lest he fall" (1 Corinthians 10:12).*

> *"Brethren, if a man is overtaken in any trespass, you who are spiritual restore such a one in a spirit of gentleness, considering yourself lest you also be tempted" (Galatians 6:1).*

Knowing your weaknesses will help to avoid being tempted.

Recognise The Triggers And Avoid Them

Let us take a quick look at some simple steps that can be taken so as to avoid being tempted.

- If your weakness is gluttony, avoid frequenting the kitchen or taking a job in a fast food restaurant or working as a kitchen porter.

- If it is lust, avoid passing by the porn magazines at supermarkets. Adopt a different route.

- It may not be wise to take up a job as a bartender if you are struggling with alcohol neither would you do yourself any favours in taking up a job at a night club if you cannot handle lust.

- I counsel that, if you are dealing with lust, you should not visit a new Christian (of the opposite sex) alone even in an emergency.

- I would also counsel that you should not volunteer to be an Usher or Treasurer for any organisation (including the Church) if you are struggling with stealing since you may have to handle money.

- If you are an impulse or emotional buyer, avoid window shopping.

Be Watchful

Three times in the Gospels, the Bible admonished us to pray not to enter into temptation.

> *"Watch and pray, lest you enter into temptation. The spirit indeed is willing, but the flesh is weak"* *(Matthew 26:41).*

> *"Watch and pray, lest you enter into temptation. The spirit indeed is willing, but the flesh is weak"* *(Mark 14:38).*

> *"When He came to the place, He said to them, "Pray that you may not enter into temptation"* *(Luke 22:40).*

Praying against temptation is to be done daily. It is part of what has been described as the Lord's Prayer. As we commit every other activity of the day into God's hands, we also need to pray against being tempted.

"Give us this day our daily bread. And forgive us our debts, as we forgive our debtors. And do not lead us into temptation, but deliver us from the evil one. For Yours is the kingdom and the power and the glory forever. Amen" (Matthew 6:11-13).

We pray daily for bread. However, that is not to be done exclusively. As we pray for our daily bread, we also need to pray daily, 'Lead me not into temptation.'

Why do we need to watch? Jesus answered,

"The spirit indeed is willing, but the flesh is weak" (Matthew 26:41).

Temptation is a struggle between the spirit and the flesh. When we pray, we communicate with our spirits but by watching, we communicate with our flesh so we can effectively deal with the inner struggle. Believe me, our flesh are weak. We need to be more discerning and not appear too spiritual. Even when we have prayed, we do not ignore the feelings, but keep watching.

Watching and praying are to be done together. One is not above the other. Some of us just pray but we do not watch. When you pray not to be tempted, you have to keep the eyes open. You cannot claim victory on the axle of prayer alone. You need to watch continually for the telltale signs of temptation. Moreover, when you see them, do not just recount or recite the scriptures or start praying, expecting they will go away. Do something.

Let me use an example. When you are watching a movie alone in the comfort of your home, hold the remote control close by. If something strange appears on your screen (as they sometimes do), do not start to pray, just change the channel. No amount of praying will change the programme. This is not the time to 'watch and pray.' Let your fingers do the watching and praying, change the dial.

On the other hand, when you are counselling the opposite sex alone or conducting a deliverance session, have someone close by and do not lock the doors. Invite a mentee or you can ask your spouse to join you. Even after you have taken all precautions, keep your eyes wide open as you pray. Watch and pray. If you are ministering to a lady and suddenly the lady's shoulder strap should loosen (as they sometimes do), you will immediately notice and you can run just as Joseph did.

Keep Your Heart Pure

The mind is in the realm of the soul. It is the seat of intellect and will. It is where the fiercest battles take place – a place the devil wants to control. So the devil may suggest things into the mind (also known as the heart, from the Hebrew word 'leb'). If you allow him to win you over in the area of your thinking, you will carry out his instructions.

> *"Above all else, guard your heart, for it affects everything you do" (Proverbs 4:23, NLT).*

At the instance of Jesus' temptations, the devil may not have appeared to Him physically. He may have only suggested a few things to His heart, but Jesus was discerning enough to recognise the plot of the evil one.

The Little Sisters of the Poor were going from door to door in a French city, soliciting alms for old people. One nun called at the house of a rich free-thinker who said he would give 1000 francs if she would have a glass of champagne with him. It was an embarrassing situation for the nun, and she hesitated. However, the hesitation was short – after all, 1000 francs meant many loaves of bread. A servant brought the bottle and poured, and the brave little nun emptied the glass. And then she said, "And now, sir, another glass please, at the same price." She got it. And the devil got her.

The devil still deploys the same strategies today. He wants to steal your heart, but you should not let him in. You should bring every evil thought into captivity to the obedience of Christ.

> "For though we walk in the flesh, we do not war according to the flesh. For the weapons of our warfare are not carnal but mighty in God for pulling down strongholds, casting down arguments and every high thing that exalts itself against the knowledge of God, bringing every thought into captivity to the obedience of Christ, and being ready to punish all disobedience when your obedience is fulfilled" (2 Corinthians 10:3-6).

When the devil suggests something contrary to the will of God, immediately replace it with God's words. That way, your actions will be godly. This should save you, but if you do not, you will eventually carry out those thoughts.

> "Don't copy the behaviour and customs of this world, but let God transform you into a new person by changing the way you think. Then you will know

what God wants you to do, and you will know how good and pleasing and perfect His will really is" (Romans 12:1-2, NLT).

"Finally, brethren, whatever things are true, whatever things are noble, whatever things are just, whatever things are pure, whatever things are lovely, whatever things are of good report, if there is any virtue and if there is anything praiseworthy – meditate on these things" (Philippians 4:8).

Draw Near To God

The second step in temptation is being drawn away. Before the enemy is ever going to succeed in destroying you, he will of necessity have to drag you away from God. As long as you are close to God in your heart, and in your actions, Satan can never succeed in overcoming you. That is not to say that he will not try, but he will never win you over. The devil is after your mind. Let me give you a simple principle: 'The closer you are to God, the farther away you are from the devil.' The converse also holds true: 'The farther away you are from God, the closer you are to the devil.' So you can conclude: if you want to be far away from the devil, draw near to God.

"So humble yourselves before God. Resist the Devil, and he will flee from you. Draw close to God, and God will draw close to you. Wash your hands, you sinners; purify your hearts, you hypocrites" (James 4:7-8, NLT).

The scriptures tell us that we may be drawn away from the simplicity and purity of devotion to Christ. The Gospel is so simple people walk away from it. If our love for God or the things of God is second place, something is wrong, and we need to be careful and return to God.

> *"But I am afraid lest somehow, as the serpent deceived Eve by his craftiness, your minds may be led astray from the simplicity and purity of devotion to Christ"* (2 Corinthians 11:3, LEB).

Enduring Temptation

John Paton was a missionary in the New Hebrides Islands. One night hostile natives surrounded the mission station, intent on burning out the Patons and killing them. Paton and his wife prayed during that terror-filled night that God would deliver them. When daylight came, they were amazed to see their attackers leave. A year later, the chief of the tribe was converted to Christ. Remembering what had happened, Paton asked the chief what had kept him from burning down the house and killing them. The chief replied in surprise, "Who were all those men with you there?" Paton knew no men were present – but the chief said he was afraid to attack because he had seen hundreds of big men in shining garments with drawn swords circling the mission station.

There are instances where you've done all there is to do but the objects that bring temptation are immovable. What more can you do? Endure.

"No temptation has overtaken you except such as is common to man, but God is faithful, Who will not allow you to be tempted beyond what you are able, but with the temptation will also make a way of escape, that you may be able to bear it" (1 Corinthians 10:13).

Sometimes it may be possible to run or walk away from certain types of temptation. There are others however with which you may not find things easy if you decide to run. Running or walking away would appear as if you are walking away from self. I'll give an example.

If you trained as a chef and have built career as a chef, how would you deal with gluttony? Walk away from your profession? No, you just endure and bear it.

How about this? If you are struggling with pornography, you have a lot to bear. They come at you from all angles; from the television to the billboards; from the public phone booths to the Internet. They are everywhere. If someone suddenly decides to build a clubhouse near your house, you can relocate. If you go to the shopping mall and you find porn magazines on the shelves, you can walk away. You have a choice to visit the beach or not to. However, there is nothing you can do when summer arrives, and people wear suggestive clothing. Are you going to hide during the summer and only come out in winter? No, you just have to endure and bear it.

That was why Apostle Paul said 'that you may be able to bear it.' Temptation places on you a heavy burden. It is like being under a weight. Though it is not physical, it can indeed be heavy. The Greek word translated bear is **hupophero**. It means to 'bear from underneath.' It means to carry a load and to endure. So you see, "you may be able to bear it."

Moreover, you can take it to Jesus. He is your burden-bearer. Whatever you cannot do for yourself, He can do for you. He said in His word,

> *"Come to Me, all you who labour and are heavy laden, and I will give you rest. Take My yoke upon you and learn from Me, for I am gentle and lowly in heart, and you will find rest for your souls. For My yoke is easy and My burden is light"* (Matthew 11:28-30).

There is a reward when we endure temptation. There is a crown when we persevere. Enduring temptation is a way of demonstrating our love for God. When we fall because of temptation, we sin against ourselves, others and God. The stories of Joseph and David clearly show this to be true. Joseph said this when he was chased by his master's wife,

> *"No one here has more authority than I do! He has held back nothing from me except you, because you are his wife. How could I ever do such a wicked thing? It would be a great sin against God"* (Genesis 39:9, NLT).

David also echoed this revelation after his extramarital affair with Bathsheba,

> *"Against You, and You alone, have I sinned; I have done what is evil in your sight..."* (Psalms 51:4a, NLT).

The crown of life is God's way of rewarding endurance.

> *"Blessed is the man who endures temptation for when he has been approved, he will receive the crown of life which the Lord has promised to those who love Him"* (James 1:12).

Chapter 9

GOD IS FAITHFUL

L et us now look at the faithfulness of God during our times of struggle.

> "No temptation has overtaken you except such as is common to man, but God is faithful, Who will not allow you to be tempted beyond what you are able, but with the temptation will also make a way of escape, that you may be able to bear it" (1 Corinthians 10:13).

Your Temptation Is Common

Whatever it is you are going through is not unusual. Because of the depth of our pain, many of us would like to think that our situation is peculiar and relish such uniqueness. We even ignore people's concern for our welfare because we feel they do not understand our struggles. Whatever name you call it, however you describe it, it is common. Your temptation is not unique. What you are experiencing has happened to someone in the past; it is happening to someone right now, and it will still happen to someone in the not too distant future.

"Be alert, be on the watch! Your enemy, the Devil, roams round like a roaring lion, looking for someone to devour. Be firm in your faith and resist him, because you know that your fellow-believers in all the world are going through the same kind of sufferings" (1 Peter 5:8-9, GNB).

"History merely repeats itself. It has all been done before. Nothing under the sun is truly new" (Ecclesiastes 1:9, NLT).

God Is Faithful

Secondly, God is faithful. God knows what you are going through, and He also knows about it. You may think God has deserted you because your circumstance remains unchanged, or there is no help from Him. He knows. He is just watching how you are handling things.

"And the LORD said: 'I have surely seen the oppression of My people who are in Egypt, and have heard their cry because of their taskmasters, for I know their sorrows" (Exodus 3:7).

God is faithful. He will not allow you to be tempted beyond your ability. He has deposited on the inside of you the ability to withstand whatever He has allowed the Devil to throw at you. You cannot fail.

"Dearest friends, you were always so careful to follow my instructions when I was with you. And now that I am away you must be even more careful to put into

action God's saving work in your lives, obeying God
with deep reverence and fear. For God is working in
you, giving you the desire to obey Him and the power
to do what pleases Him" (Philippians 2:12-13, NLT).

Even when we fail or falter, that will not change God's personality.

"If we are faithless, He remains faithful; for He cannot
deny Himself" (2 Timothy 2:13, NLT).

God Allowed It

Thirdly, whatever you are going through is permitted. God allowed it. You are tempted with permission. God would never tempt you. It is Satan's job to tempt you, and he cannot tempt you until he has God's permission.

"...Who (God) will not allow you to be tempted
beyond what you are able" (1 Corinthians 10:13).

Did you notice the word 'allow?' If you are facing any challenges now, it is because God allowed it.

Satan is a vagabond. After first assigning responsibilities to members of his team, Satan just walks about looking for scapegoats to destroy. Moreover, the Bible says the devil walks around 'seeking whom he may devour.' The Bible did not say he devours anyone he seeks; only seeks those whom he may devour, perhaps he will find one.

"Be sober, be vigilant; because your adversary the devil walks about like a roaring lion, seeking whom he may devour" (1 Peter 5:8).

"Now there was a day when the sons of God came to present themselves before the LORD, and Satan also came among them. And the LORD said to Satan, 'From where do you come?' So Satan answered the LORD and said, 'From going to and from on the earth, and from walking back and forth on it.' Then the LORD said to Satan, 'Have you considered My servant Job, that there is none like him on the earth, a blameless and upright man, one who fears God and shuns evil?' So Satan answered the LORD and said, 'Does Job fear God for nothing? Have You not made a hedge around him, around his household, and around all that he has on every side? You have blessed the work of his hands, and his possessions have increased in the land. But now, stretch out Your hand and touch all that he has, and he will surely curse You to Your face!' And the LORD said to Satan, 'Behold, all that he has is in your power; only do not lay a hand on his person.' So Satan went out from the presence of the LORD" (Job 1:6-12).

There Is A Limit

Fourthly, there is a limit, a cap on your suffering. Let me remind you again what that scripture says.

"Who (God) will not allow you to be tempted beyond what you are able" (1 Corinthians 10:13).

"'Behold, all that he has is in your power; only do not lay a hand on his person.' So Satan went out from the presence of the LORD" (Job 1:12).

God has put a cap on your sufferings based on the grace of endurance you have been given. Again I say to you; you can handle it. Concerning Job, God told Satan, "There is a boundary you must never cross." Satan said, 'Yes Sir,' then left.

God will not allow you to be tempted beyond what you are able. That means you have the ability. Even if you doubt yourself, God can trust you. Your temptation has a limit. It will not go beyond a certain limit – your ability. No temptation can be overpowering. So make sure you do not fall.

There Is A Way Of Escape

Finally, there is a way of escape. To be perfectly honest, God will always provide an escape route when the challenges seem overwhelming and overpowering. The problem with many of us is that we are so caught up in our afflictions to the point we have been blinded to the many escape routes God provides.

Look for the exit sign; there is always one. There are situations you do not need to pray or even ask questions. Three times in the scriptures we are admonished to take to our heels against the temptation of immorality, love of money, and lust.

"Flee immorality. Every other sin that a man commits is outside the body, but the immoral man sins against his own body" (1 Corinthians 6:18, NASB).

"But flee from these things you man of God and pursue righteousness, godliness, faith, love, perseverance and gentleness" (1 Timothy 6:11, NASB).

We are admonished to flee from youthful lust.

"Run from anything that stimulates youthful lust. Follow anything that makes you want to do right. Pursue faith and love and peace, and enjoy the companionship of those who call on the Lord with pure hearts" (2 Timothy 2:22, NLT).

BOOK 2

Good Finish
To Bad Start
Life is not an experiment – it is a choice!

TOTAL FREEDOM

CONTENTS

Introduction

DON'T SELL OUT

I want to tell you the story of the prodigal son. The story can be found in the Gospel according to Luke, chapter fifteen, and verses eleven through to thirty-two.

There was a wealthy man who had two sons. The younger demanded to have his inheritance while his father was still alive.

> *"In this case of a will it is necessary to prove that the person who made it has died, for a will means nothing while the person who made it is alive; it goes into effect only after his death" (Hebrews 9:16-17, GNB).*

Against his wish and the customs of the elders, the father gave unto him a portion of the inheritance.

The young man packed his bags and travelled to the ends of the earth and squandered his future. At his destination, the economy became depressed and the standard of living went up. Things became unaffordable so he started living rough. After a long time of suffering alone, he decided to hook up with a citizen so they could share the mounting burden together. Things grew even worse and he began to feed on pod meant for swine on the field where he got a part time job. When he could no longer bear the pain of hard life, he came back to his senses and decided to swallow his pride and return home as a servant.

He returned home hoping to work and be paid just like any servant in the house but ran into the embrace of his waiting father who with good grace offered him pardon.

The lives of many people today resemble that of this prodigal. When they should be pursuing worthwhile projects, they run after immediate and temporary gratification.

The devil still uses the same strategies today. He has not changed. He often convinces people it's not necessary to be serious about the things of God. He lulls people into a fake sense of security and makes believing God look stupid.

He is in the business of stopping people making their destiny. He will use money, sex, fame, pride, laziness, illness, and whatever else is available at his disposal to make sure people do not fulfil their destiny.

He will try to convince people that using drugs, taking alcohol or smoking is okay. He will tell people it is okay to have sex before marriage or be unfaithful to their spouse saying something like this: "after all God is merciful and compassionate, He sure will forgive if you repent". From taking such risks, many people have met with their end without repenting.

He finally targets the heart or soul. He makes people fear the future. He uses worldly pleasure and hopes of wealth to enslave people. Today, many people's god is money and their church is work. But God says,

"No servant can be the slave of two masters; such a slave will hate one and love the other or will be loyal to one and despise the other. You cannot serve both God and money" (Luke 16:13, GNB).

Over the past twenty years, I have seen a number of my Christian friends drop out of the race. They got trapped in the futile pursuit of worldly pleasures. Many started Christian fellowships, others pioneered churches, while others joined existing vibrant congregations. There was fire burning in their bones. They required no convincing to do any assignment. They were unstoppable. We organised outreaches together, played in the Christian Football League and won three successive victory trophies. We joined together in organising our weddings and receptions. We were going to take the city for Jesus.

Unfortunately, one by one they dropped off, their flames extinguished. I have watched how out of frustration, loss of focus and the devil's distractions, many of my friends have abandoned the passion and commitment they used to have. They lived like they had eternity to enjoy and would never grow old or weary.

But I have good news for you. This book is written to encourage those who have given up hope concerning their future not to give up. You may have had a poor start but you can still have a good finish. You can still rise up, better your life, and help the generation coming behind.

This is not a book for the fainthearted or those who just want to pass through life as statistic. It is a book for the brave, bold, courageous and spirited; those who want to live life knowing time is redeemable but life is irreplaceable; those who are not waiting for life to happen to them but are ready to take it by the horns and ride on the platform of living than just existing.

Though life deals them a great blow, they muster their energy to get back up and face life again.

I encourage you to carry on reading if you are ready to take charge of life by the help of God. Adam failed to take charge of life and he lost dominion in the Garden of Eden. Cain did not take charge of his life; he became a murderer and a wanderer. Noah and Abraham took charge and they impacted their world. If you must finish well, you need to take charge of the rest of your life. Have a good read.

Chapter 1

MAXIMISE THE MOMENT

Friends of George Burns have always kidded him about his singing. Burns, a master of self-deprecating humour, decided to take advantage of this and insure his voice for a million dollars. He thought it would be a wonderful publicity stunt. "I was so excited," said Burns, "I couldn't wait to rush down to the insurance company. I took a cassette and a tape recorder with me so the insurance man could hear my voice. It was one of my best numbers – a syncopated version of Yankee Doodle Blues with a yodeling finish. The insurance man listened patiently to the whole thing, and then he just looked at me and said, 'Mr. Burns, you should have come to us before you had the accident.'"

George Burns was too late.

Who you are today could be a result of what happened to you yesterday. What you will become tomorrow could be determined by the choices you make today. What happened yesterday may not be your fault but what you become tomorrow is your responsibility. You can blame somebody for pushing you down but you can only blame yourself for staying down. Whatever you sow, you will reap. So, what you do today will affect your tomorrow.

A farm boy accidentally overturned his wagonload of corn in the road. The farmer who lived nearby came to investigate.

"Hey, Willis," he called out. "Forget your troubles for a spell and come on in and have dinner with us. Then I'll help you get the wagon up."

"That's mighty nice of you," Willis answered, "But I don't think Pa would like me to."

"Aw, come on, son!" the farmer insisted.

"Well, okay," the boy finally agreed, "but Pa won't like it."

After a hearty dinner, Willis thanked his host. "I feel a lot better now, but I just know Pa is going to be real upset."

"Don't be foolish!" exclaimed the neighbour. "By the way, where is he?"

"Under the wagon."

Many people leave their problems under the wagon and pursue after temporary pleasures. They miss their opportunity.

Born With A Silver Spoon

I looked at the top 10 richest men in the world in October 2012, and like many years before, only 2 of them made their wealth from inheritance. Four-fifths were self-made. It's true to say that no one is born rich.

> *"After all, we didn't bring any money with us when we came into this world, and we can't carry away a single penny when we die"* (1 Timothy 6:7, TLB).

Job said,

> *"I was born with nothing, and I will die with nothing" (Job 1:21, GNB).*

Whether you were born in a royal or general hospital, naturally or with help of surgery, in a developing or developed nation, all of us were born naked and empty. We all brought nothing into this world; all of us in this sense are equal. So we can say God is good and very impartial.

No one is born with a silver spoon in their mouth. Those who inherited wealth were given silver spoons after they are born into families of people who laboured ahead of them to acquire the spoon and accumulate the wealth.

Millions of people live in and by the legacy of their parents' fortunes. But there's nothing like becoming a "self-made" man. Very few people read books written by people who inherited their wealth but books written by self-made millionaires are instant best sellers.

All Are Equal

> *"Whatever you do, do well. For when you go to the grave, there will be no work or planning or knowledge or wisdom. I have observed something else in this world of ours. The fastest runner doesn't always win the race, and the strongest warrior doesn't always win the battle. The wise are often poor, and the skillful are not necessarily wealthy. And those who are educated don't always lead successful lives. It is all decided by chance, by being at the right place at the right time. People can*

never predict when hard times might come. Like fish in
a net or birds in a snare, people are often caught by
sudden tragedy" (Ecclesiastes 9:10-12, NLT).

Work now because when you die, you cannot work anymore. That's the message in the passage and the summary of the tenth verse. Coming to verse eleven, we can say; making it in life has little to do with our swiftness, strength, intelligence, wit, or how good we are. The fastest runner doesn't always win the race, and the strongest warrior doesn't always win the battle. The wise are often poor, and the skillful are not necessarily wealthy. And those who are educated don't always lead successful lives. Doesn't that sound familiar? Let me remind you what it concludes:

"... It is all decided by chance, by being at the right
place at the right time" (Ecclesiastes 9:11, NLT).

That sounded like a contradiction. If making it in life is a result of right positioning and right timing, it suffices to say that it cannot be left to chance. So for the rest of this section, we will try to understand this statement and see how it applies to our lives.

The word 'chance' used in this passage may be a little confusing. I say this because it will suggest uncertainty. It may also suggest coincidence. This is not what it means. God is not a God of chance or of coincidences. Everything He does is preordained and planned. The statement 'by being at the right place' means things do not happen accidentally or randomly. If you are not at the right place at the right time, you might miss your chance.

The Hebrew word translated 'chance' is the word *'pega'* which means occurrence or happening. It speaks of an incident or event rather than an accident. It is from the root word *'paga'* which means; to encounter, meet, reach, entreat, or make intercession.

An alternate word would be 'opportunity.' So from now on I will be using the word 'opportunity.' Let's now replace the word 'chance' with the word 'opportunity' in the NKJV and see how it reads:

> *"I returned and saw under the sun that – the race is not to the swift, nor the battle to the strong, nor bread to the wise, nor riches to men of understanding, nor favour to men of skill; BUT TIME AND OPPORTUNITY HAPPEN TO THEM ALL. For man also does not know his time: like fish taken in a cruel net, like birds caught in a snare, so the sons of men are snared in an evil time, when it falls suddenly upon them"* (Ecclesiastes 9:11-12, Emphasis mine).

If agility, strength, wisdom, education or ability does not make a person, what will? My answer is simple; TIME and OPPORTUNITIES. What makes the difference between your making it in life or otherwise is how you spend your time and take advantage of the opportunities that come your way. This is why I said earlier on that God is fair. He is good and impartial. No one will stand before Him in judgement to say he didn't make it because he was not born into a rich family or nation. The worlds 10 richest billionaires used their time and opportunities wisely to create or increase their wealth. Most are from poor families and nations and represent all age groups. Some did not have a good start, but they changed their fortunes by seizing the moment. They were not going to settle for a bad start and a bad finish.

Since we came to this world with nothing, God gave us time and opportunities fairly. If you pay close attention to how you spend your time and grab the opportunities that God brings your way, you will be fulfilled and make it in life.

What An Opportunity?

God gives to everyone a measure of time and plenty of opportunities. Within your time frame, there are ample windows of opportunities. We don't create opportunities for ourselves; God does, using other people. You can desire it but you cannot create it. After you desire it, you wait patiently for it. When it arrives, you jump at it.

It is like a surfer. He doesn't create the waves. All he does is get ready, and wait for the waves. So you have to be prepared and be watchful for your divine opportunities.

Winners know that so-called 'luck' is the intersection of preparation and opportunity. They appear to be fortunate because their positive self-expectancy enables them to be better prepared for their opportunities. If an individual is not prepared, he may not see or take advantage of an opportunity.

Opportunities abound, but only those who are prepared utilise them effectively. When asked by a news reporter how she thought she would do in one of her early career swimming events in the United States several years ago, 14-year-old Australian Shane Gould replied, "I have a feeling there will be a world record today." She went on to set two world records in the one hundred and two hundred meter freestyle events. When asked how she thought she would fare in the more testing, gruelling, four hundred meter event, Shane replied with a smile, "I get stronger every race, and besides ... my parents said they'd take me to Disneyland if I win, and we're leaving tomorrow!" She went to Disneyland with three world records. At 16 she held five world records and became one of the greatest swimmers of all time, winning three gold medals in the 1972 Olympics. She learned early about the power of self-expectancy.

No opportunity comes to the un-expectant. If the opportunity comes, he may not recognise it. God is not going to ask someone to sow a car into your life if you don't have a driver's license. You have to show your desire by your readiness. Are you prepared for what God is about to do in your life? Preparation is a sign of expectation. For the Christian, the expectation is in sight.

> *"For surely there is an end; and thine expectation shall not be cut off" (Proverbs 23:18, KJV).*

One morning a man went out to start his car to go to Church. Flat tyre, no problem, he had a spare. He changed the tyre quickly and went on his way. He didn't think to drop the damaged tyre off to be fixed. "I'll get around to it," he said. Within five days, he went to get the car to go to school. Another flat! Only this time no spare! He had to roll it to the nearest station and waited while it was fixed. When something breaks, fix it now. Don't wait until you need it and then you don't have it! The man did not expect another puncture so he did not prepare.

Some people have had wonderful waves of opportunities and wasted them because they were scared to jump into the deep. Inadequate preparation can cause fear. Fear can cripple expectation and low expectation means inadequate preparation. It becomes a cycle. If you are going to make it in life, you have to take risks. Risk is what keeps a potential winner at bay and unprepared. Winners see risk as opportunity. They see the rewards of success in advance. They do not fear the penalties of failure. Those that succumb to fear become critics of those that do not. After they miss their opportunities, they start to criticise those who took advantage of theirs; those who have jumped into the sea of opportunities, making money, growing Churches, buying houses and making indelible marks. Fear can paralyse to the point where you submit to just getting-by. This attitude will never guarantee a good finish. For you to succeed in life, you need to doubt your doubts and replace your fear with faith.

The opportunity that is presented to you puts value on your time. Without opportunity, time is useless. For instance, if someone places a demand on your time without giving you advance notice, releasing that time for them will indicate how much value you place on your time.

Chapter 2

GOD KNOWS YOUR TIME

God knows the years He has apportioned for everyone and the number of years we are supposed to stay here on earth; we don't. He has it all written in His diary.

"For You formed my inward parts; you covered me in my mother's womb. I will praise You, for I am fearfully and wonderfully made; marvellous are Your works, and that my soul knows very well. My frame was not hidden from You, when I was made in secret, and skillfully wrought in the lowest parts of the earth. Your eyes saw my substance, being yet unformed. AND IN YOUR BOOK THEY ALL WERE WRITTEN, THE DAYS FASHIONED FOR ME, WHEN AS YET THERE WERE NONE OF THEM. How precious also are Your thoughts to me, O God! How great is the sum of them! If I should count them, they would be more in number than the sand; when I awake, I am still with You" (Psalms 139:13-18, Emphasis mine).

You came to earth as an answer to someone's request. Someone has a need so God fashioned you to meet that need and sent you to earth on a divine assignment. You are important to God. You are not a spectator; you are a major player in God's scheme of life. God then apportions the number of years you will require for the assignment to be completed and this is recorded in His book. In the same way, God knows exactly how long it will take me to fulfil His vision for my life on earth and so gives me all the years that are needed to do the task.

This is the good part of it: as long as you are in the will of God for your life, you cannot die before your years are completed and the job accomplished. The devil will try to weaken, discourage, or even attack you but you cannot die until your assignment is completed.

When you say you do not have time for something, it means one of three things:

1. You are trying to do what was never part of God's plan for you;

2. You have already wasted God's allocated time doing what was outside His will for you;

3. Or it is not His appointed time for that thing to be accomplished.

For instance, if I couldn't find time to write this book it would mean either of three things: God didn't ask me to write it so there was no time allocated for writing this book in His diary; I might have wasted my time doing other things He never intended for me to do; or the writing of the book is in the future.

God does not give everyone the same number of days or years; He gives sufficient time to get the job done. He allocates our days depending on our assignment. As in the physical, the time it will take for any job to be completed will depend on the nature of the job. Some may take many days and some few days or even years. Fulfilling the number of your days in God's reckoning is not as important as finishing the assignment and finishing well.

Master your time. It is the currency of life. This is one of the things God gave everyone equally. People who are making impact have not been given more time than you. They have only maximised it in a way it can profit them. If you spend your time wisely you will finish well. Spend it foolishly and you have yourself to blame. Do the right thing at the right time and you will quickly notice the profit it will bring to you.

There Is Time For Everything

"To everything there is a season, a time for every purpose under heaven: a time to be born, and a time to die; a time to plant, and a time to pluck what is planted; a time to kill, and a time to heal; a time to break down, and a time to build up; a time to weep, and a time to laugh; a time to mourn, and a time to dance; a time to cast away stones, and a time to gather stones; a time to embrace, and a time to refrain from embracing; a time to gain, and a time to lose; a time to keep, and a time to throw away; a time to tear, and a time to sew; a time to keep silence, and a time to speak; a time to love, and a time to hate; a time of war, and a time of peace. What profit has the worker from that in which he labours? I have seen the God-given task with which the sons of men are to be occupied. He has made everything beautiful in its time. Also He has put

eternity in their hearts, except that no one can find out the work that God does from beginning to end. I know that nothing is better for them than to rejoice and to do good in their lives, and also that every man should eat and drink and enjoy the good of all his labour – it is the gift of God. I know that whatever God does, it shall be forever. Nothing can be added to it, and nothing taken from it. God does it that men should fear before Him. That which is has already been, and what is to be has already been; and God requires an account of what is past" (Ecclesiastes 3:1-15).

The Hebrew word translated time is the word 'et.' In its general use, it means a period of time, an appointed time, a proper time or season. 'Et' connotes time conceived as an opportunity or season as in a fixed, set time or period. It is also used secondarily of the concept of proper or appropriate time or suitable time as for the time God has appointed for one to die or carry out a given activity in life. A third use of the word connotes a season or a regular fixed period of time such as springtime, harvest time, time of life, rainy season, period of the day and so on.

In the Greek language there are three main divisions of time: *chronos* – where we get chronology; *Kairos* – which means season; and *hora* – which is translated hour. Time is an event while season is a series or periods of events. The hours of each day make up the seasons and the seasons make up our years. There are seasons of events within the time we are born and the time we die. The number of our days is a length of time while the events in our lives occur in seasons. The days measure the quantity while the season measures the quality. So Solomon begins the chapter of one of his books by saying everything has a purpose, a time and a season.

> *"To everything there is a season, a time for every purpose under heaven: a time to be born and a time to die" (Ecclesiastes 3:1-2).*

For every full measure of life there are three seasons: a morning season, an afternoon season and a night season, and each season is presented with lots of opportunities.

Chapter 3

The Morning of Life

Paul said,

"When I was a child, I spoke as a child, I understood as a child, I thought as a child; but when I became a man, I put away childish things" (1 Corinthians 13:11).

How spot on that scripture is? Paul said that a child speaks first before he understands and then thinks. If you see someone who speaks before understanding or thinking, that person is like a child. But then Paul became 'a man.' You have to 'become' a man. Age is not an indicator of maturity. Some say that you mature with age. This may not always be true. People can be mentally retarded or physically less able though they are grown-ups. You are only a child once but can be forever immature. You do not suddenly begin to think unless you first "become." It is a gradual but non-guaranteed process. You can be physically matured but be mentally retarded.

This is also true of Christians. There is countless number of people in Churches who are immature though saved for a long time. Their Church attendance record can be a hundred percent yet their spiritual temperature can be very low. They have full understanding of Church liturgy but a scanty Christian library. All their Christian lives, they have been feeding on milk and have refused to grow up. You'll find such people attend evening sessions at conferences instead of day sessions where they can study the word of God. They have made many preachers' pockets fat. Call a soul winning event, they will never come. Invite a motivational preacher and they'll call sick to work. Evening sessions where I had been motivational in my approach were always packed compared to the day teaching sessions. The only exception are those by the nature of their professions may not be given time off to attend morning meetings.

To grow up spiritually, you have to feed on real food, not milk. You have to 'become'. We all started life as babies but we cannot remain babies. The only two people that started life as grown-ups were Adam and Eve.

Jesus also was born as a baby in a manger. Then,

> "Jesus grew up in wisdom and stature and in favour
> with God and all the people" (Luke 2:52, NLT).

When Jesus became of age (12 years old), He made a decision to think no longer like a baby. He was assumed to have been following the relatives on their way back from an annual Passover festival but He was gone to Church.

> "Three days later they finally discovered Him in the
> Temple, sitting among the religious teachers,
> listening to them and asking questions. All who heard
> Him were amazed at His understanding and His
> answers. His parents didn't know what to think.
> "Son," His mother said to Him, "why have You done

this to us? Your father and I have been frantic, searching for you everywhere." "But why did you need to search?" He asked. "Didn't you know that I must be in my Father's house?" But they didn't understand what He meant. Then He returned to Nazareth with them and was obedient to them. And His mother stored all these things in her heart. Jesus grew in wisdom and in stature and in favour with God and all the people" (Luke 2:46-52, NLT).

Jesus was first spiritually matured before he was physically matured. He grew up first in wisdom before adding stature; "Jesus grew up in wisdom and stature."

Even His parents could not catch up with His level of understanding; "But they didn't understand what he meant." He questioned their lack of understanding when He asked "Didn't you know I must be in My father's house?"

He also dazed the religious teachers with His level of understanding; "All who heard Him were amazed at His understanding and His answers."

All these happened before Jesus became a teenager. He then matched up His spiritual maturity with physical growth. He had to snatch Himself up from people's expectation. In other words, He 'became'. You do not have to remain a baby Christian; you too can 'become.'

To 'become' involves a deliberate definite decision. This stage before you 'become,' corresponds to the morning of life. It is the foundation stage where a lot of work needs to be done. Whatever happens, careful attention needs to be given and paid to this stage. The future of every person is shaped at this stage.

"If the foundation be destroyed, what can the righteous do?" (Psalms 11:3). Simpler renderings of this verse say: "The foundations of law and order have collapsed. What can the righteous do?" (Psalms 11:3, NLT); "There is nothing a good person can do when everything falls apart" (Psalms 11:3, GNB).

If this stage of life is not carefully structured with God's guidance, a man may live the rest of his life trying to correct the past. Even the righteous (God-fearing, God-loving, prayerful man) will have a challenge. "What can the righteous do?" David asked.

This is a stage when a child is built-up. It is a life formation stage where the child learns to trust people, formulates a worldview, develops habits, struggles with life's meaning, develops their creativity, copes with demanding school work, peer pressure, has identity crises, speech and language formation, or struggles with sexuality. There is a lot going for them at this stage. So we are admonished to,

"Teach children how they should live, and they will remember it all their life" (Proverbs 22:6, GNB).

This stage is also the dependence stage. A child at this stage depends on others for supply, support, strength, and safety – supply when in need; support in the pursuit of their aspirations; strength when weak; and safety when vulnerable. They lean on their parents, carers as well as guardians; on teachers as well as governments.

Sometimes parents and carers do a good job at bringing them up. Unfortunately, many do not. Because children are not allowed to choose for themselves, the onus is on us to make wise decisions on their behalf. It is rather unfortunate that the future of many have been destroyed by bad leadership of parents and carers. Many innocent children have become victims of bad governance, circumstances, and the environment in which they grew up. As a result of missed opportunities many people have been condemned to a life sentence of robbery, child labour, drug abuse, child prostitution, gun crimes, and abuse in many other forms, ranging from sexual to mental abuse and other mishaps due to no fault of their own.

"We missed him. Our chance to change things came and passed and we did not know it was there." A little boy sat through Sunday School classes for three years at a great Baptist Church (First Church, San Antonio) but someone missed him. His name was Sirhan Sirhan, and at age 24 he shot and killed Senator Robert Kennedy. In a welter of words and the shudder of grief throughout the nation, the persistent thought keeps recurring...someone missed him," said Dr. Jimmy Allen.

The Bible puts this age group around birth to twenty or twenty-five years. By age twenty five people are treated as a fully grown, responsible adult. They are not expected to take major responsibilities before they turn twenty. There are twenty one Bible references instructing men to be enlisted for service when they reach twenty. Here are just a few of them.

> "You and Aaron are to take a census of the people of Israel by clans and families. List the names of all the men twenty years old or older who are fit for military service'" (Numbers 1:2-3, GNB).

> "The LORD said to Moses, 'From the age of 25 each Levite shall perform the duties in the Tent of my

presence, and at the age of 50 he shall retire. After that, he may help his fellow-Levites in performing their duties in the Tent, but he must not perform any service by himself. This is how you are to regulate the duties of the Levites'" (Numbers 8:23-26, GNB).

The children of Israel are expected to pay offering as 'ransom money' when they reach twenty. They are not expected to pay this money before age twenty as their parents did that on their behalf. But at twenty they are expected to start working and be able to afford such offering. At twenty they also contributed to the building materials for the Tabernacle. That was expected because they could work.

"Everyone included among those who are numbered, from twenty years old and above, shall give an offering to the LORD" (Exodus 30:14).

"A bekah for each man ([that is], half a shekel, according to the shekel of the sanctuary), for everyone included in the numbering from twenty years old and above, for six hundred and three thousand, five hundred and fifty [men]" (Exodus 38:26).

The Israelites were also considered innocent before they turned twenty. God commanded those that were twenty years and older to be killed so they don't pollute the younger ones.

"The carcasses of you who have complained against Me shall fall in this wilderness, all of you who were numbered, according to your entire number, from twenty years old and above" (Numbers 14:29).

This is my point. According to the Bible, any person below twenty is considered young. They are innocent and should not have to work. So the responsibility of their care lies with parents, guardians or government authorities. This is a big responsibility which should not be taken lightly. Today, the work age has been drastically widened, between 16 and 75 years.

> *"I have singled him (Abraham) out so that he will direct his sons and their families to keep the way of the LORD and do what is right and just" (Genesis 18:19, NLT).*

> *"Teach your children to choose the right path, and when they are older, they will remain upon it. Just as the rich rule the poor, so the borrower is servant to the lender" (Proverbs 22:6-7, NLT).*

> *"And now a word to you parents. Don't keep on scolding and nagging your children, making them angry and resentful. Rather, bring them up with the loving discipline the Lord Himself approves, with suggestions and godly advice" (Ephesians 6:4, TLB).*

> *"Now I am coming to you again, the third time; and it is still not going to cost you anything, for I don't want your money. I want you! And anyway, you are my children, and little children don't pay for their father's and mother's food – it's the other way around; parents supply food for their children" (2 Corinthians 12:14, TLB).*

"Good people leave an inheritance to their grandchildren, but the sinner's wealth passes to the godly" (Proverbs 13:22, NLT).

The best we can do for our younger generation is not just to leave them money or wealth. What they need is for them to know God and be known by God. When they have God, they will have money. Without leading them in the way of the Lord, they will waste the wealth we give them. If they are taught the way of the Lord, then they will be good stewards of God's resources. We have to get this priority right.

We can also bring up our children by commanding, directing, teaching, disciplining, training, providing and giving them godly advice. This is our duty of care and it is an enormous responsibility. We can best do this through modelling. What we do speaks volumes to them, more than what we say.

We can also get them the right education if we can afford to. If we do, we would have given them the right to choose. Remember, education gives people information but cannot make wise people. Education cannot make people successful but it provides them a choice. Let us work hard at getting them the right education so they can be free to go whichever way they choose without limitations.

We need also to help our children in channeling their energies creatively. We can help them to build good, lasting friendships and trust. As future leaders we need to help them to develop good morals, godly habits, issues of sex and sexuality, the meaning of life and right world views. We owe them this due diligence.

As soon as people slip out of this age group without good foundation, though they might have attained physiological maturity and physical independence, they can remain mentally bound by their past or upbringing. They resign themselves to what is called NFA (No Future Ambition) or choose to be wild, loose, and become a grade two NFA (No Fixed Address). Of course, without education and good skills, what else can they do? We do not want our children to end up as NEET (No Education, Employment or Training). We want them to be neat, clean, and valuable members of our quickly abating societies.

Maybe you are already feeling that your own life is being described and you think life has short-changed you. Do not despair, there is hope. Your past may not be your fault, but what you do with your future is entirely your choice. Your start may be bad but you can have a good finish.

It was 1818 in France. Louis, a boy of 9 years was sitting in his father's workshop. The father was a harness-maker and the boy loved to watch his father work the leather.

"Someday father," said Louis, "I want to be a harness-maker, just like you."

"Why not start now?" said the father. He took a piece of leather and drew a design on it. "Now, my son," he said. "Take the hole-puncher and a hammer and follow this design, but be careful that you don't hit your hand."

Excited, the boy began to work, but when he hit the hole-puncher; it flew out of his hand and pierced his eye! He lost the sight of that eye immediately. Later, sight in the other eye failed. Louis was now totally blind.

A few years later, Louis was sitting in the family garden when a friend handed him a pine cone. As he ran his sensitive fingers over the cone, an idea came to him. He became enthusiastic and began to create an alphabet of raised dots on paper so that the blind could feel and interpret what was written. Thus, Louis Braille opened up a whole new world for the blind – all because of an accident!

Louis was an accident victim who refused to condemn himself and be a burden on his carers. He decided to change his life and those of many like him. He had a bad experience but a good finish.

My late dad is another good example. He came from a family that was poor. His father was a peasant farmer and so was his mother. They could not afford to pay for his education.

At an early age, he sacrificed his education for work. From his meagre wages he managed to send his siblings to school one by one. Dad also saved up to take care of his father and pay for private tuition for himself up to his first degree.

Dad pursued his teaching career to the point of becoming the Vice-Principal of a college and shortly before his appointment as the Principal of another college he was invited to serve the state government in a bigger capacity.

From grass to grace! That is what best describes him. He went from zero to become a hero. He was appointed a State Commissioner by two successive political governments during two different regimes. Dad travelled the world, used the best cars, and lived in fantastic accommodations.

As a godly man, he was appointed the head chief of the Chieftaincy Council in his hometown, a post which remained empty four years after his demise. He sponsored all his children up to university and my mum didn't have to work after she was 45. Dad died in service at the age of 69 and received a State burial in recognition of his contribution to the welfare and development of the State. The ceremony took place at the largest city Cathedral covered by the local and national media. He was buried in style. He was born a pauper, but buried a prince.

My dad did not condemn himself. You should not. He could have spent his entire life building blame bricks on his parents who though tried their best, could not help their son. He just tried to make the best out of the rest of his humble existence and his efforts were very well rewarded.

As a child of God, there is no technical knock-out in this battle. You can still get up and be somebody in life. Let's just suppose your morning was rough; your parents really tried to educate you but couldn't make ends meet. You even tried to help yourself but it proved too difficult. Do not allow your past to become the obstacle against your future. Forget what could have been and focus on the present and the future.

> "No, dear brothers, I am still not all I should be but I am bringing all my energies to bear on this one thing: FORGETTING THE PAST AND LOOKING FORWARD TO WHAT LIES AHEAD" (Philippians 3:13, TLB Emphasis mine).

> "Make good use of every opportunity you have, because these are evil days" (Ephesians 5:18, GNB).

You don't have to condemn yourself to a life sentence of lack or failure. You may not be able to recover the past but you can redeem the future. Welcome to your afternoon!

Chapter 4

THE AFTERNOON OF LIFE

The morning of life is the laying of foundations while the afternoon of life is the building stage. It is the time for building a home, not an edifice. Building a house is important but secondary to building a home. It is the stage where to get married and start having children. It is also a stage of building a career, a profession and then buying houses. This is the stage when things begin to solidify and set in stones. What people do at this stage in life will stay with them for the rest of their life.

The people in this age group sustain the airlines. They are the ones going around the world shopping for business. This age group keeps the economy buoyant. If you pull them out of employment, the economy of any nation, no matter how strong, will collapse. They are the largest group in employment.

This group also sustains the housing market. When someone get past this age group, they may have to deposit twice or sometimes more as down-payment for a property as a first time buyer.

> *"We admire the strength of youth and respect the grey hair of age" (Proverbs 20:29, GNB).*

Young people have a lot of strength but for many of them unfortunately, what should have been an asset is deployed on unprofitable ventures now working against them. Rather than utilise their privileged positions and God-given resources to procure their future, youths tend to see their energy as something that will never diminish. They forget that time is God-given and opportunities are divinely orchestrated. Wasted opportunity means wasted time and more wasted opportunities and time. The cycle is never ending.

With a lot of energy and money, these 'city boys' (as they are sometimes described) travel the world partying and engaging in all forms of activities of temporal value. Instead of securing a future for themselves and their families, they squander, misuse and sometimes abuse their opportunities. They dissipate their energy and fritter away their future.

They call it enjoyment. Others call it youthful exuberance. It is misplaced priorities and a waste of time. Something within says to them: "You are still young, if you don't enjoy now, you can't enjoy when you are older. Don't let any man (or woman) lock you in the prison of marriage, enjoy your life" (as if being married is bondage). "If you have children now, you won't be able to enjoy freedom anymore." "Why buy a house now, you are only twenty five; why not wait? You won't have money anymore to spare. Without disposable income, you won't be able to afford nice things just like your peers."

None of the above is true. Marriage is not bondage. Though it is fraught with many challenges, it is still the first and best institution God created. Despite the rising divorce statistics, many unmarried people want to get married and widows, widowers and divorcees rush to remarry. What is responsible for this? I do not know. But I think the idea is that being married is good. I am not suggesting that you should rush into marriage but there are a lot of benefits and advantages if you marry early.

It is equally untrue that having children early takes away your freedom or liberty. It may appear to be so at the beginning, but it is rewarding and fulfilling all the same. The joy you have when the children grow up and are semi-independent or independent is immeasurable. If they do well in life, the parents are thrilled and show them off to their friends. It even sounds selfish to consider any child as a burden on the parents. You should dispense your energies on your children than on anything else. At the end of the day, your family will be all you have left. Same can be said of owning your own home while you are still young.

"Enjoy a little, travel a little, and put your tomorrow on pause?" If all you do is squander the financial resources God gives you, you may have been deceived. For Jesus said,

> *"We must work the works of Him who sent Me and be busy with His business while it is daylight; night is coming on, when no man can work" (John 9:4, AMP).*

Moses also echoed the same sentiment when he said,

> *"Seventy years are given us! And some may even live to eighty. But even the best of these years are often emptiness and pain; soon they disappear, and we are gone. Teach us to number our days and recognise how few they are; help us to spend them as we should" (Psalms 90:10, 12, TBN).*

Moses said we are to live for 70 and possibly 80, but they are nothing. 'So Lord teach us to number (not count) our days'. Why? In order "That we may apply wisdom." When we celebrate our birthdays, we count the length of our days. But Moses did not ask us to count the length of our days, he asked us to number them. When we number our days, it gives us an idea of how they have been spent and how far away from 80 we are. Counting our days is about quantity while numbering our days is about quality.

Some people live while others exist. If we are to live rather than just exist, it starts with being in the centre of God's will for our lives and if by 70 or 80 we could not find fulfilment, then we have just existed. So God gives to each of us a specific number of days or years to live. Though we count our years in upward increments, we really should be counting down. As we grow in years, we get physically older. We start to die from the day we make our earthly entry. So Moses said "…so we can apply wisdom." Wisdom is what we need to live right.

In life, we don't often get one opportunity twice. We always think we have more than one 'chance.' No, it is not true. We may have another chance or another opportunity to do what should have been done before. It is always another chance, never the same one twice. To have the same opportunity, we would need to rewind time or God may have to extend our days to accommodate the lost time or reschedule our assignment. I mean, cut down our earthly assignment.

Having a second or third chance is not even the norm, it is an exception. So don't miss your opportunities. That may prove expensive. Don't squander it. Seize the moment and maximise the opportunities. If you believe the devil that says 'you still have your whole life ahead of you,' you might have sold your birthright and future to him just as Esau did to Jacob.

If you buy now and postpone the payment, you may pay more dearly and direly for it in the future. You can choose to enjoy life now and pay for it later or you can choose to sacrifice your pleasures and comforts at this time so you can enjoy later. This is called delayed or deferred gratification. It is possible to have a good start but end woefully. However, it is better to have a good start and have a good finish. Your better can become bad if it prevents you from your best. What you call your present 'best' can be 'bettered'. There is so much more ahead of you. Don't even settle for the best – reach higher, there is always more ahead.

Just Imagine

- A twenty five year mortgage paid off; your last child graduating from the university when you are 50; and retiring from actively running your own business as you have been doing for the last twenty five years.

- You don't have to go to work because of a mortgage at age 50. You stop changing nappies at 32 years of age. Or you have control over your time as a company director at twenty five years of age.

- Sitting on a 500% returns by the age of 50, or leaving home without having to worry about baby sitters when you are 40, or re-setting your own salary every year if you so wish.

Did you notice the figures 25 and 50? That's right. I have done that deliberately to say this,

"The LORD said to Moses, 'From the age of 25 each Levite shall perform the duties in the Tent of my presence, and at the age of 50 he shall retire. After that, he may help his fellow-Levites in performing their duties in the Tent, but he must not perform any service by himself. This is how you are to regulate the duties of the Levites'" (Numbers 8:23-26, GNB).

You could say that Bill Gates fulfilled this scripture, retiring as the CEO of Microsoft at an early age to focus on things more dear to his heart. At the age of 50, we should retire from active labour. So says the Bible. We are from then supposed to participate in supportive roles. But if the divinely allocated time and opportunities have been missed, you may have to work longer and harder to make ends meet. When will you then have time for God?

This worried David so much that he inquired of God to tell him how many days have been allocated to him to live on earth.

"Please, LORD, show me my future. Will I soon be gone? You made my life short, so brief that the time means nothing to you. Human life is but a breath, and it disappears like a shadow. Our struggles are senseless; we store up more and more, without ever knowing who will get it all" (Psalms 39:4-6, CEV).

Grabbed Or Missed Opportunities

I became a Church leader within a year and a half of joining my fellowship. I started attending a new believers' class called BBC (Believers' Bible Class) straightaway. I joined the class as a student although I had been born again ten years before but had never been through a structured teaching on the basics of the new birth.

After the session which lasted 3 months, I was invited by our teacher to assist him during the next class session. I had thought I would be an usher helping to make the class conducive for studies. I soon realised it was in a teaching capacity after he asked me to prepare to lecture him on one of the curriculum subjects at his house.

He was so impressed by my presentation that after he introduced me as his new assistant, he never came back to the class. Not that he left the Church; he just took a risk at trusting God, my teaching gift, and skill. From then on I became our Church's BBC teacher. Within months, I also launched the BBC course at other branches and became the National BBC Coordinator.

It was my opportunity. I saw it and grabbed it. As soon as I was asked by my teacher to make the presentation, I did not fret or refuse the offer. Not that I had done it before in that capacity but I was willing to give it my all. (Of course I was a teacher and a tutor before relocating to England). I fasted and prayed. Then I studied the subject until I almost became an authority on it. I researched as if it was a thesis. I bought books and revised hard just on this one subject.

Why did I go to that length? It was my opportunity and I did not want to miss it. From then on, my promotion was rapid – from a non-stipendiary BBC teacher to the full-time denomination's Bible College Provost, in just five years. My quest and thirst for God led me to a further study at a Bible College in the UK. I do not yet know as I should but I keep learning and finding out. Whatever God achieved with me, He can with you.

One day many years ago a bright boy found employment in a photograph gallery in Nashville, Tennessee. His wages were small, but he took good care of them, and in the course of time he had saved up a snug little sum of money. One day a friend less thrifty than he came to him with a long face, and asked for a loan of money, offering a book as security. Although the other knew there was little probability of his ever being repaid, he could not refuse the request. 'Here is the money; keep your book and repay me when you can.'

The grateful lad went away in such haste that he left the book behind. The kind youth examined the volume with curiosity. It was a work on astronomy, by Dick, and it so fascinated him that he sat up all night studying it. He had never read anything which so filled him with delight. He determined to learn all that he could about the wonders of the heavens. He began thenceforth to read everything he could obtain relating to astronomy.

The next step was to buy a small spy-glass, and night after night he spent most of the hours on the roof of his house studying the stars. He secured, second hand, the tube of a larger spy-glass, into which he fitted an eye-piece, and sent to Philadelphia for an object glass. By and by he obtained a five-inch (130mm) glass retractor telescope, which, as you know, is an instrument of considerable size.

Meanwhile he worked faithfully in the shop of the photographer; but his nights brought him rare delight, for he was never tired of tracing out the wonders and marvels of the worlds around us. With the aid of his large spy-glass he discovered two comets before they were seen by any of the professional astronomers, whose superior instruments were continually scanning the heavens in search of the celestial wanderers. This exploit, you may well suppose, made the boy famous. He was invited by the professors in Vanderbilt University to go thither and see what he could do with their six-inch telescope. He never graduated from the school, but he did receive the only honorary degree Vanderbilt had ever awarded. In the course of the following four years he discovered six comets. He was next engaged by the Lick Observatory. With the aid of its magnificent instrument he discovered eight comets, and astonished the world by discovering the fifth satellite of Jupiter, Amalthea. He invented a new method of photographing the nebulae in the Milky Way, and has shown an originality approaching genius in his work in star photography.

Perhaps you have already guessed the name of this famous astronomer, which is Prof. Edward Emerson Barnard in charge of the Yerkes Observatory of Chicago University, and this is the story of how he worked up. If you are ever going to climb the ladder of finishing well where only few dare to, you need to keep learning and remain focused on the object.

In 1991 Thomas Dexter, a country preacher met with Sarah Jordan Powell (the noted gospel singer known as the songbird of the Church of God in Christ) at a small dinner conference. The meeting provided Dexter the long awaited opportunity to invite this national Fine Arts Director of the second largest Pentecostal denomination in the world (who also happened to be a well-travelled gospel singer with eight albums to her credit) to minister in song in one of his services while he preached. The trip to West Virginia provided an opportunity for Powell to marvel at the preaching of Dexter.

Like most black preachers nationwide, Dexter knew about the Azusa Conference held yearly in April and was impressed by the fact that his new ally was a close friend of the host. A year after Powell visited his Church, Dexter called to inform her of his plan to attend the next Conference. After the evening session of the second day Dexter finally realised his ambition to meet the Conference host having been introduced by his new acquaintance. At the meeting, a taped message of one of Dexter's meetings was forced into the hands of the Conference host.

After listening to the tape and with a little persuasion from Powell, Dexter was invited by Carlton Pearson later in the year to keynote mini-Azusa, a regional meeting of ministerial leaders of the Azusa fellowship held at Higher Dimensions, Pearson's home church alongside two other ministers, Mark Hanby and Brian Keith Williams. Pearson decided to play segments of Hanby, Williams and Dexter's sermons preached at the ministerial leaders' meeting on his television program, and his production staff took great care to edit them down to seven-minute clips portraying each preacher at his best.

A seven-minute clip from an hour long message titled 'Behind Closed Doors' was only a third of a day slot on a TV airing contract Pearson had with a Christian broadcasting network. By sheer coincidence (or rather, God-incidence), the President and founder of the network happened to tune to his own network after a tiring day of intense contemplation. It was at this time the programme was being aired – at the very minute the best seven minutes of the message was being aired.

As it happened, Paul Crouch, the founder of Trinity Broadcasting Network (TBN) was writing his autobiography 'I had no Father but God' at the time. Answers to some of the questions he was asking came listening to Thomas Dexter Jakes speak on this fateful day. Paul immediately inquired about this unknown guest preacher, requested the entire message, and aired it full length every Friday for the next eight weeks.

In February of the following year, Pearson invited T.D. Jakes back to Higher Dimensions – this time on a Sunday. Jakes preached his now classic sermon, 'The Puppet Master,' delineating how God works behind the scenes for believers in a manner resembling a puppet master pulling strings. A few weeks later, Pearson decided to call Jakes to invite him to speak at the main event, the Azusa Conference in April. After his experience with Paul Crouch playing his message on TBN, Jakes was no longer naïve about what television exposure could do for his career. He knew that many Azusa services were aired live on TBN, and since he had previously impressed Crouch, another classic sermon could produce tremendous momentum for his budding fame.

What do you preach to make a profound impact at Azusa 93? Well, Jakes decided to preach 'Woman, Thou Art Loosed,' a sermon that was sparked by his successful Sunday school lessons back in West Virginia. The auditorium was jam-packed on the closing night of the conference. Pearson had to tell the workers to pull down the curtains to make more seats available to the waiting audience as they were beginning to be turned away. As a result 12,000 people came in that night to hear Jakes. That simply was it. The rest as they say is history. That was a grabbed opportunity; just one woman, Sarah Jordan Powell, and the expectant Jakes.

Don't miss your opportunity. This is the time. This is the moment. It is the time to serve God and serve Him wholeheartedly. This is the time to make money, and lots of it. Save a lot and invest or start your own business. It is the time to build or buy your house. It is the time to marry and start a family, have all your seven children quickly.

It reminds me of the story of two salesmen sent to a country with a few shoes. On arrival they discovered that nobody wore shoes. It meant their few stocks were already too many. One of them called to his company to come and get him out of the country but the other requested for more stock. Their reason was the same, "No one wears shoes here." One of them saw obstacles and impossibilities but the other saw opportunities and possibilities.

Many people see big challenges and run away from what can be the big opportunities of a lifetime. They see problems and obstacles in every opportunity but winners and successful people see opportunities in every problem.

The army of Israel saw Goliath as an obstacle but David saw him as his opportunity to demonstrate God's awesome power and he eventually became the undisputed monarch in Israel. They saw the Philistine as being too big to hit, but David saw him as too big to miss. That was his opportunity.

In like manner, the ten spies saw the Philistine giants as unbeatable but the two spies Joshua and Caleb saw them as too small for their Jehovah God. They were the only two spies who made it to the Promised Land.

Many times we miss our opportunities because we look at the enormity of our challenge rather than the bigness of our God.

Some years ago an energetic young man began work as a clerk in a hardware store. Like many old time hardware stores, the inventory included thousands of dollars' worth of items that were obsolete or seldom called for by customers. The young man was smart enough to know that no thriving business could carry such an inventory and still show a healthy profit. He proposed a sale to get rid of the stuff. The owner was reluctant but finally agreed to let him set up a table in the middle of the store and try to sell off a few of the oldest items. Every product was priced at ten cents. The sale was a success and the young fellow got permission to run a second sale. It, too, went over just as well as the first.

This gave the young clerk an idea. Why not open a store that would sell only nickel and dime items? He could run the store and his boss could supply the capital. The young man's boss was not enthusiastic. "The plan will never work," he said, "because you can't find enough items to sell at a nickel and a dime." The young man was disappointed but eventually went ahead on his own and made a fortune out of the idea. His name was Frank Winfield Woolworth.

Years later his old boss lamented, "As near as I can figure it, every word I used in turning Woolworth down has cost me about a million dollars!"

If you are an employee reading this book, go back to work tomorrow and ask your boss to throw challenges your way. It may lead you to the discovery of your life – something you may never realise were it not for the challenge. If you are given an unusual task like tidying the kitchenette, don't just tidy it up; get a towel and gloves, and clean it up as if it were your house and your real paid job. Perhaps someone will notice the difference and give in a good word to your employer for you. Don't say you cannot do the job because it's beneath you.

If you are a potential employee required to make a ten minute presentation at an interview, do it as if it was a major international seminar. Give it all your best, study, research and get help to prepare your slides. That may be your opportunity.

If you serve in a Church and your pastor gives you a responsibility, don't say it belongs to a different department. Of course, your pastor knows. It's your opportunity to shine; just do it. If nobody else notices you, God does and will reward your willingness and humility.

Jacob was not preparing the red stew for Esau. He was preparing it for himself but he made it palatable enough for someone else to desire it. Don't do things shabbily either because it's yours or because it's not yours. Someone might be watching and take interest. When Esau asked for the stew, Jacob had his opportunity and grabbed it. He was ready. If he was not ready, he could have missed the birthright outright.

Minimise the Movement

Grab the moment. God brings the opportunity; all you need to do is get ready to grab it. Who knows when it will come? Don't mess around; use your energy wisely to your advantage. Stay focused on your career, job or profession. Don't jump from one job to another every six months. It's the time, it's the moment, don't let it slip by. You are not going to remain the same forever. Vigour diminishes; strength wanes; so use yours to the maximum. When you take hold of the moment, you take hold of the future. If you ok today, it may affect your tomorrow. Today was yesterday's tomorrow and your tomorrow will soon become today. Time waits for no man, so grab the moment. Minimise the movement, maximise the moment.

> *"Even those who are young grow weak; young people can fall exhausted. But those who trust in the LORD for help will find their strength renewed. They will rise on wings like eagles; they will run and not get weary; they will walk and not grow weak"* (Isaiah 40:30-31, GNB).

Chapter 5

THE EVENING OF LIFE

The evening of life is the consolidation stage when previous work and labour starts yielding interest. No mortgage to pay and less stress to face. This is when an individual becomes his own boss. It is a time all the children should have graduated from University or college. Some of the children may even be married. As to leisure, the evening of life is a time to travel around the world and enjoy the views.

Unfortunately, this is also the time of diminished vigour. Gradually failing health may mean that some things may become a struggle. Things that used to be straightforward and easy when someone is younger can become very tasking and daunting. Running up the stairs, running after buses, and jumping around with grandchildren, are a few of them.

One more thing; a person in the evening of life may be less employable. He may not be able to compete with twenty five year olds for a number of jobs except where many years of experience are required.

The question I get asked by many people at this stage of resting is this: "If my afternoon season was horrible, what do I do with my life now that I am old and aged?"

If you are in this age group, do not think you are condemned. It is not my intention to do so. I just want to challenge the youth enough so as to prevent them from wasting their lives but make the best of their God-given potentials and maximise this season.

Now to the answer: no life is useless. Someone once said that age is in the mind. You are only as old as you think. I have seen many people of age achieved more than the younger ones. Abraham was called to a life of absolute devotion to God when he was 75. Another example is Moses who started his ministry when he was 80. And one of his disciples, Caleb took on a new project when he was 85.

> "...Look at me! I am eighty-five years old and am just
> as strong today as I was when Moses sent me out. I
> am still strong enough for war or for anything else"
> (Joshua 14:10-11, GNB).

Let us take a look at older people. It is generally believed that older people exist only to enjoy their old age. It sounds like they are whiling away the time waiting for the day of their death. Yes, they do enjoy the fruits of their labour, but they have not necessarily finished their assignment on planet earth. When Jesus finished His assignment, He was crucified. When Paul finished his assignment, he was killed.

You are not sustained on earth to kill time. In God's plan, old people are kept on earth to produce more fruit. When an old person ceases to be fruitful they will be called home. Fruit bearing for the righteous continues until death. Bible retirement is from active administrative responsibilities, not from ministry.

> *"They shall still bear fruit in old age; they shall be fresh and flourishing" (Psalms 92:14).*

You think the time is gone? No. There are many good things about being old. Most people will get old if Jesus tarries anyway. Rather than be afraid to grow old, you should begin to plan for that time.

The richest place on earth is not a geographical location somewhere. It is at the back yard. It is at the graveyard where billions are buried with their gifts and talents. It's such a sad waste. There is more in you than you think; a lot more that can still benefit millions. Don't die with them. You were loaded with gifts when you were born. Your gifts are for people here on earth. You should not go to the grave with anything God purposed for the benefit of others. You should not die full but empty. Empty yourself. The more you do for God, the better your end.

The last assignment my dad had with the state government started when he was 65 years old. Not that there were no younger and more agile aspirants; he just had the experience required for the post. He did not even vie for it; he was appointed. The government discovered something in him and demanded it.

Even if it appears that the degeneration of the physical body is taking its toll on you, it should not be a reason or excuse to stop being active in the things of God. While you engage in the less physical side of living, you are very valuable in ministry to younger minds. Use the little strength left in you to serve the One who created you until He says it is time to quit.

> *"Be watchful, and strengthen the things which remain…" (Revelation 3:2).*

God is in the business of restoration and redemption. When we think about restoration, we always think in terms of physical things alone. On the other hand when we think about redemption, we often think in terms of spiritual things. Neither is the complete truth. God can restore physical as well as spiritual losses. In a similar manner, He can redeem losses in the spiritual and material. Do not worry about the years you've lost and how hopeless your situation may seem; God can and will redeem and restore them back to you. Your latter rain and the former rain can fall in the same month.

> *"See then that you walk circumspectly, not as fools but as wise, redeeming the time, because the days are evil" (Ephesians 5:15).*

> *"So I will restore to you the years that the swarming locust has eaten, the crawling locust, the consuming locust, and the chewing locust, My great army which I sent among you" (Joel 2:25).*

One of the many good things about getting old is that you have a lot of experience on your side. This is also known as life's school.

> *"The glory of young men is their strength; of old men, their experience" (Proverbs 20:29, TBL).*

Experience (good or bad) is one of the reasons we need older people around. We can learn from either. We can also learn from personal experiences. I once heard it said that 'only a fool doesn't learn from his own experience.'

A story is told of a young man by name Rehoboam who sought the advice of the elders who stood before his father Solomon while he was yet king. Rehoboam asked, "How do you advise me to answer these people?" The whole assembly of Israel had gone to ask Rehoboam to lighten their yoke. After asking the elders, Rehoboam also inquired of the young men on the same issue. They gave opposing advice to that of the elders.

Rehoboam rejected the advice of the elders but embraced that of the young men. Rather than relieve them, he added to the people's yoke. And that was the beginning of his end. Listen to what the people said to Rehoboam;

> "What share do we have in David, what part in Jesse's son? To your tents, O Israel! Look after your own house, O David! So the Israelites went home" (1 Kings 12:16, NIV).

For ignoring the wisdom of the aged, the Israelite dynasty became divided during the reign of Rehoboam as foretold by prophet Ahijah the Shilonite. The entire story is told in 1 Kings, chapters 12 and 13.

The saying holds true that "Though the young may outnumber the aged on new clothes, never can the aged be outnumbered on old ones." When the young falls, he looks forward, but the aged look backwards. Older people look to see what made them fall and learn from it but if you look forward when you fall, you probably will fall again on the same issue because you haven't looked for the reason why you fell. That is what is called experience. When we move close to the elderly, they can help us with their experience of the past for our future.

Older people have lots of understanding too. From the experience they have acquired through the years, understanding has been developed. Understanding is a sign of maturity. It distinguishes boys from men, children from adults, and young from elderly.

> *"Dear brothers and sisters don't be childish in your understanding of these things. Be innocent as babies when it comes to evil, but be mature and wise in understanding matters of this kind"* (1 Corinthians 14:20, NLT).

The NKJV puts it this way "... but in understanding be men" (1 Corinthians 14:20).

Having understanding is just as important as pursuing after wisdom. You cannot get wisdom without first having understanding. Solomon did not only pray for wisdom, he prayed for understanding as well. With understanding, God granted him wisdom, riches, honour and length of days.

> *"... Therefore give to Your servant an understanding heart to judge your people...Then God said to him, 'Because you ... have asked for yourself understanding to discern justice, ... I have given you a wise and understanding heart, ... riches and honour'"* (1 Kings 3:1-14).

Wisdom without understanding is a dangerous weapon in the hands of a youth. Solomon was given wisdom and understanding, but he promoted wisdom and underplayed understanding. With his wisdom Solomon ended up with 300 wives and 700 concubines. He lost understanding and made many mistakes which cost him the kingdom – though not in his own lifetime. Therefore the Bible enjoins us not only to pursue wisdom, but also to get understanding – which is what aged people have.

> *"Wisdom is the principal thing, therefore get wisdom. And in all your getting, get understanding"* *(Proverbs 4:7).*

Get close to the elderly and draw understanding from them. Having understanding will give you better life.

> *"Understanding is a wellspring of life to him who has it. But the correction of fools is folly"* *(Proverbs 16:22).*

Glossary Of Understanding From The Book Of Proverbs

> *"A wise man will hear and increase learning, and a man of understanding will attain wise counsel"* *(Proverbs 1:5).*

> *"Discretion will preserve you; understanding will keep you"* *(Proverbs 2:11).*

> *"Happy is the man who finds wisdom, and the man who gains understanding"* *(Proverbs 3:13).*

"Hear, my children, the instruction of a father, and give attention to know understanding" (Proverbs 4:1).

"Say to wisdom, 'You are my sister, and call understanding your nearest kin" (Proverbs 7:4).

"Wisdom is found on the lips of him who has understanding, but a rod is for the back of him who is devoid of understanding" (Proverbs 10:13).

"Good understanding gains favour, but the way of the unfaithful is hard" (Proverbs 13:15).

"Wisdom rests in the heart of him who has understanding, but what is in the heart of fools is made known" (Proverbs 14:33).

"He who has knowledge spares his word, and a man of understanding is of a calm spirit. Even a fool is counted wise when he holds his peace; when he shuts his lips, he is considered perceptive" (Proverbs 17:27-28).

"Counsel in the heart of a man is like deep water, but a man of understanding will draw it out" (Proverbs 20:5).

"A man who wanders from the way of understanding will rest in the assembly of the dead" (Proverbs 21:16).

Chapter 6

NOW IS YOUR TIME

What we spend time on is an indication of where our priorities lie. We live in a world where priorities have been misplaced. People are their own gods. Most people are self-centered and selfish and lack any respect for authority or other people. Knowing and placing a value on certain priorities in life will help to determine how to manage and maximise your time. Your friends and family members want some of your time too. Setting priorities will help to allocate the time of the day in such a way that it can be maximised. Let me share with you how to manage your time based on biblical priorities.

Put God First

Priority number one is assigned to God Almighty. In all you do, acknowledging God is of utmost importance. No one can have a good finish without God's backing. If we take a look at the Ten Commandments you will notice that the first four commandments concern our relationship with God. They are found in Exodus 20:1-11 and Deuteronomy 5:6-15.

1. You shall have no other gods before me.

2. You shall not make for yourself an idol.

3. You shall not misuse the name of the Lord your God.

4. Observe the Sabbath day by keeping it holy.

Many people wrap God around their little fingers. They say things like 'If I am not at work and I have time, I will go to Church.' They ought to say 'if I don't have Church, I'll do this and that.' This is not to say that we should not work. It means we only do that which is required and put God first before we agree to an extra shift or overtime. We must first establish what carries a greater priority: more work or God.

Time with God should be foremost and non-negotiable. This includes time to pray, time to study God's word, fellowship with brethren and attend Church. If God is more important, then He must be first. The Bible says we should seek God's kingdom first.

> *"But seek first the kingdom of God and His righteousness, and all these things shall be added to you" (Matthew 6:33).*

Jesus demonstrated this when He challenged His parents about their knowledge of His mission.

> *"'Why were you searching for Me?' He asked. 'DON'T YOU KNOW I had to be in My Father's house?' But they did not understand what He was saying to them" (Luke 2:49-50, NIV).*

No twelve-year old dares challenge their parents that way now! Jesus was telling His earthly father that there was a Higher Father. Now, if I were Joseph, that would have upset me. It's like a son telling his step dad that someone is more important than him. Yet He was not being rude. He was just stating a fact that should have been obvious – God is number One – a Creator far more important than His creation.

Later, Jesus also turned to His brothers and sisters. This is what He said,

> *"'Who are My mother and My brothers?' He asked. Then He looked at those seated in a circle around Him and said, 'Here are My mother and My brothers! Whoever does God's will is My brother and sister and mother'"* (Mark 3:33-35, NIV).

What a shock! His family must have either thought He had gone out of Himself or admit He knew what He was doing.

As if that was not enough, Jesus also turned to His disciples and said,

> *"If you want to be My follower you must love Me more than your own father and mother, wife and children, brothers and sisters – yes, more than your own life. Otherwise, you cannot be My disciple"* (Luke 14:26, NLT).

The point is this. In all His dealings, Jesus showed there was none more important than God, the Heavenly Father. He is Number One. I must admit, putting Him first in my life hasn't come easy. It is a daily crucifying of the flesh. It may demand going on missions when you'd rather go to Miami on holiday; reading your Bible when you'd rather read a novel; praying when you'd rather talk to friends; fasting when you'd rather feast. Putting God first means there are places we cannot go, things we cannot say, things we cannot look at, and saying sorry even when you've been wronged. It means we have to put our desires secondary to God's will. Now you say that is not easy? No, it is not, but this we must do if we are to put God first.

You Are Next

You come next. This is a difficult one for most humble believers to accept. The Bible does not teach that we should put other people first. No one can do that; otherwise he would be a hypocrite. Airlines tell us to first look after ourselves in the unlikely event of an emergency. The reason is that I will be of no value to anyone if I am of no good to myself. How can I help other people unless I have been helped? Whenever we find people taking this position, we make them feel guilty unnecessarily. We call them names: selfish, self-centered, and egocentric because they won't give to us. However, the fifth of the Ten Commandment is centered on our welfare. Let us read it in the Old and New Testaments.

> *"Honour your father and your mother. Then YOU will live a long, full life in the land the LORD your God will give YOU" (Exodus 20:12, NLT).*

> *"Honour your father and mother – which is the first commandment with a promise – that it may go well with YOU and that YOU may enjoy long life on the earth" (Ephesians 6:2-3, NIV).*

Nothing could be simpler. To dishonour ones parents is suicidal.

"For God said, 'Honour your father and mother' and 'anyone who curses his father or mother must be put to death'" (Matthew 15:4, NIV).

Many lives have been shortened and many have been sent to an early grave for having disregarded this injunction by God. I must emphasise however that the first reason to honour your parents is your welfare. Put it this way: After God, you next, then others.

Let us look at one more New Testament verse. The entire Old Testament is summarised in this verse.

"Jesus said to him, 'You shall love the LORD your God with all your heart, with all your soul, and with all your mind.' This is the first and great commandment. And the second is like it: 'You shall love your neighbour AS yourself.' On these two commandments hang all the Law and the Prophets" (Matthew 22:37-40, Emphasis mine).

Love your neighbour AS yourself? Notice that verse said you are to love your neighbour 'as yourself,' not above yourself, not in place of yourself.

"Be kindly affectionate to one another with brotherly love, in honour giving preference to one another" (Romans 12:10).

In preference, you can decide to offer your space to someone. Even after you have given that space, it remained your space that you gave away. You are inferior to none and no one is superior to you. When you prefer your brother's comfort to yours, you are simply honouring him.

We make people who would not give beyond the biblical requirement feel less holy or even unrighteous. So they give with their hands but not with their hearts.

Let me share with you the story of Ananias and Sapphira in the Book of Acts. The announcement went forth like this, "Brethren, we need your help to look after the needy amongst us. These people are new converts who have turned their backs on the world to follow Jesus and we won't let them down. Nothing is too big or too small." Then the donations started flooding in; big ones, small ones, expensive ones, cheap ones, clothes, shoes, foods, and many more. You name it; everything was brought.

The simple call soon turned to something else, 'fund-raising extraordinaire.' It became a competition. Who would bring the best? Who would offer the most? So people started selling their boats, horses, houses, and landed properties. Those who held on to their houses, contrary to people's expectations were made to feel less spiritual.

Soon entered a couple, "Minister, guess what? We sold our land." "Really, for how much?" replied the minister. (Of course the minister knew about property prices and was in the boat business himself). After he was told the price, the minister shouted "you liars."

Bang! Ananias fell on the floor and died. A few hours later, Sapphira 'conspirator-wife' also went down on the floor. She was declared dead on the spot, just like her husband. They died because they lied about the value of the money declared against the profit they made on the sale. They did not die because they did not sell their property, neither were their deaths a result of not giving all the equity they made on the house. This is what the minister said;

"The property was yours to sell or not sell, as you wished. And after selling it, the money was yours to give away" (Acts 5:4, NLT).

No, they didn't have to sell their house. It appears that they were not compelled to do that as much as they were not forced to give any of the equity on the house. The money was theirs to keep if they wanted to but as soon as they made up their minds to give it, they couldn't lie about its worth.

It's in your power whether or not to release what belongs to you. Do not allow people to put you on guilt trip because you did not give to satisfy their ego. You only give because you are being led by the Holy Spirit to give, not because you want to prove you also can give substantially.

Looking after 'number one' (after you have fulfilled your responsibilities to God) involves spending good time looking after yourself outside your savings. You must create time to refresh and replenish – taking regular holidays for instance, just to engage in the mundane. That includes spending quality time with those dearest to you – your spouse and children. It is also a time to play, eat out, watch TV, listen to music, and read good clean fictional stories. Many people haven't done that for a long time. All their lives, they have been spending their time looking after other people's interest, putting others first.

You need to look after yourself. Your time is now. I am not talking about wasting time. I am saying that you should take reasonable, responsible, and sensible breaks. Even Jesus left the crowd to rest. He would notice a gathering crowd and think it was time to leave. This is a lesson our generation need to learn.

Looking after number one also includes your responsibilities to your parents and even your relatives. No one can teach this value better than Jesus and Apostle Paul.

> *"But you say it is all right for people to say to their parents, 'Sorry, I can't help you. For I have vowed to give to God what I could have given to you.' You let them disregard their needy parents. As such, you break the law of God in order to protect your own tradition'" (Mark 7:11-13, NLT).*

> *"But anyone who won't care for his own relatives when they need help, especially those living in his own family, has no right to say he is a Christian. Such a person is worse than a heathen" (I Timothy 5:8, TLB).*

Allow me to make this emphasis again – your time is now: to serve and service yourself. If you keep serving and servicing others without stepping aside every once in a while to replenish and look after your own interests, you will soon end up needing help like those you are helping. Life is about giving and receiving. If you keep giving without receiving, you will soon be depleted. Your resources will soon be used up and you may not even find help from those you helped. So take time off to look after yourself.

Other People Next

Let us go back to the Bible. Commandments six to ten are for others. From Exodus 20:13-17 or Deuteronomy 5:17-21 we deduce the following:

6. You shall not murder.

7. You shall not commit adultery.

8. You shall not steal.

9. You shall not give false testimony against your neighbour.

10. You shall not covet.

> *"For the commandments, 'You shall not commit adultery,' 'You shall not murder,' 'You shall not steal,' 'You shall not bear false witness,' 'You shall not covet,' and if there is any other commandment, are all summed up in this saying, namely, 'You shall love your neighbour as yourself.' Love does no harm to a neighbour; therefore love is the fulfilment of the law" (Romans 13:9-10).*

You would not want to commit adultery with your neighbour's wife or husband if you claim to love him or her. Neither would you murder your neighbour, steal his property, bear false witness against him or covet his belongings. You would not like someone that says he loves you to do any of those to you either. You would think he is a hypocrite because what he professes is not in line with his action. The last five commandments are summarised in the statement, 'You shall love your neighbour as yourself."

We have a major assignment to the less privileged. Jesus did not turn a blind eye to the needs of people. He only stepped aside to refresh and later return to ministry. He helped them and we should. If we do not, our religion is irrelevant and unacceptable.

"Pure and undefiled religion before God and the Father is this: to visit orphans and widows in their trouble, and to keep oneself unspotted from the world" (James 1:27).

My point here is this: your ministry is divided into three. There is ministry to God and there is ministry to your neighbour and right in the middle of that is your responsibility to yourself and your immediate family. God will never ask that you should place the ministry to your neighbour above your ministry to yourself and your family. In actual fact, the requirement before you minister to others is to first show your ability to manage your home. Therefore, other people come after you and your family.

You are probably feeling better already, but if that is because you've been looking for excuses not to give or bless others, then you've got me wrong. This is not a book to encourage you to block the flow of God's blessing to you. If you stop giving, the flow of material blessing will be hindered. I want you to give not for man's award but for God's reward. The Bible is full of God's wonderful promises and rewards for extending God's goodness to others.

"And let us not get tired of doing what is right, for after a while we will reap a harvest of blessing if we don't get discouraged and give up. That's why whenever we can we should always be kind to everyone and especially to our Christian brothers" (Galatians 6:9-10, TLB).

"Feed the hungry and help those in trouble. Then your light will shine out from the darkness, and the darkness around you will be as bright as day. The

LORD will guide you continually, watering your life when you are dry and keeping you healthy, too. You will be like a well-watered garden, like an ever-flowing spring. Your children will rebuild the deserted ruins of your cities. Then you will be known as the people who rebuild their walls and cities" (Isaiah 58:10-12, NLT).

"Be generous, and you will be prosperous. Help others, and you will be helped" (Proverbs 11:25, GNB).

When I speak about others, they include your Church family, friends, neighbours, work colleagues, business partners, study group, and extended family members.

The conclusion is this: if you have your priorities in the proper perspective, you will take good advantage of the opportunities God brings your way. Do not let your opportunities slip by because you feel obligated to serve others. The time is now. Your time is now. Maximise the moment.

BOOK 3

Your Basket, Kneading Bowl, And Barn

Discover the Hidden Secrets of the Affluent

CONTENTS

Introduction

Something is wrong somewhere. I do not get it. Non-Christians do seem to be having things easy; having babies they do not want, buying houses we cannot afford, riding cars we crave are ours, and growing businesses.

Poverty is not what the Bible teach. It says in Psalms 35:27,

> *"Let them shout for joy and be glad, who favour my righteous cause; and let them say continually, "Let the LORD be magnified, Who has pleasure in the prosperity of His servant."*

God is not happy when we suffer. He feels pain when we do. He has the pleasure in prosperity, not in pain.

There is a story I read in 2 Kings 4:1-7 about how God cancelled a woman's debt and gave her abundance. It tells about a prophet-in-training who answered the call to full-time ministry. In those days, there were no pastors, only prophets and priests and their call was full-time.

This prophet would depend on the faithful giving and generosity of the congregation. If they gave much, he would have much, but if they gave little, he would have little. There was no extra income from any other source. The wife was not supposed to work so she could look after the home. Today, most pastors have to work if they are ever going to keep body and soul together and some pastors' wives do, to keep the home.

This prophet-in-training came home hoping to get some rest and attend to the family, but that was going to be tricky. Just as he sat down to dinner, both the mobile and the home phones started ringing. If he does not quickly leave home to see Mr. & Mrs. Problem, he is going to lose them to another prophet.

So he left the two boys with the wife while he attended to other people's issues, and we wonder why prophets' children turn out the way they do. Such a very hardworking prophet – always there when needed. He was God fearing, very faithful, dedicated and hardworking. He never left his job and never abandoned his duty. But, he was poor.

Without help, the prophet resulted into using credit cards, overdrafts, and bank loans to supplement his pitiful salary. At least no one knew about his financial turmoil as long as the prophet was alive to pay back the loan. No one! Except the wife, perhaps. It was meant to be a secret. Prophets do not have people they can confide in - at least not the congregation.

One day, as if it were a dream, the prophet slept and did not wake up. The weight of the mounting debt, the stress of lack, the burden of the ministry, and the pressure of the workplace crushed him up. It was all too much for him to bear.

It was a sudden death; sudden unexpected departure. The prophet was a young man. He had two young children. Though they were old enough to go to the neighbours to borrow jars, they were too young to marry. The little strengths they had was only good to become slaves. This prophet was one of the sons of the prophets. Elisha was his senior prophet.

And there was the prophet's wife who inherited a massive debt due to her husband's sudden demise. If she were able to work before, she could not anymore, especially with two boys to bring up on her own. What can a single mother of two do to support her family? Whatever assets they had was not sufficient to repay their debt and the equity on their home was not enough to pay the creditors. Taking one child was not good enough; the two innocent boys had to be traded as slaves of the 'master,' the creditor.

Oops, did I say master? Yes, the borrower is a slave of the lender (Proverbs 22:7). I will tell you how. When you borrow, you work to pay back the principal. At the same time, you work to pay off the interest. Paying off the interest means you are working for the creditor. Because of his borrowing, this prophet was already a slave and his children were going to be enslaved.

The woman's husband represented her source of income. He was the bread winner and their livelihood. Well, that was taken from her. Her past and present were taken. It suddenly dawned on her that she was about to lose her future. Her children were her prospects for the future.

What could the congregation do? I sympathise. At least they have been faithful in small. Though not much all the time, they still did their best. After all, they had their own issues. Some lost their jobs; others lost their homes. That was why there was so much tension everywhere. They too were in debt.

It's our little secrets. The pastor is in debt and the members are in debt. Who is going to help us? To make matters worse, the creditors are not Christians. Our masters are non-Christians. That is the problem. Where do we go? The unsaved are after our buildings and our church vans. They are coming to get us. We are supposed to be Christians, children of the Most High God. This is ridicule, we need a miracle.

So the widow woman cried out. Why won't she? She would rather lose her mind than lose her children. She had to call for help, and God showed up.

All of a sudden, like from nowhere, in the midst of a hopeless situation, the man of the hour showed up. He did not appear empty handed but came to save the family from doom. He gave divine solution to a terrible situation.

This is what this book is about. If you would take time to digest it, you would find divine ideas that will deliver you from financial captivity. They are practical. Chapter after chapter, I discussed; my reasons for believing that poverty is a choice; how the world financial system is designed to enslave you and keep you enslaved; how to avoid its trickery; how to be delivered; and how to turn your life around and help other people with your wealth. It can be done.

What you are about to read in this book is not conventional. It is out of the box thinking, pragmatic and may seem controversial. To benefit from the teachings in this book, you need to be open minded as I have been in writing about the subject.

Come on, grab a pen and take notes, and you will be amazed what God will do shortly.

Chapter 1

YOUR BASKET, KNEADING BOWL, AND BARN

Many people focus on the concept of 'giving and receiving' as the only way to prosper, yet forget that it is only one of many ways God want His children blessed. Giving is fantastic. I have received some incredible benefits from extending my resources to other people. Giving unlocks and releases the flow of the fruits of blessing in the life of the giver.

However, this form of living limits the plan, purpose, and power of God in a believer's life and ignores the endowment deposited in him or her. Most people living by the principle of 'sowing and reaping' have a form of fundraising to make up for the usual shortfall.

I encourage ethical work as another channel for wealth transfer to God's children. God has promised to bless the works of our hands. Ethical work is encouraged throughout scripture while idleness is discouraged. It goes without saying that God himself worked. Jesus worked. Paul in the bible worked. Diligence is a bible doctrine. On the other hand, sweat is a curse, and a burden is an affliction.

On a higher dimension, I challenge you to get yourself a 'kneading bowl.' If you are employed, the kneading bowl is your side investment added to your employment income. Some may prefer to call it business or something that brings in extra income. Jacob, our main character in the book had a side investment as he served Laban.

Your basket is your employment income, your kneading bowl is your investment income, and your barn is your savings, which is also a form of investment or asset.

Keep the scriptures that follow at the fore of your heart as you read the rest of this book. The Holy Spirit will provide inspiration as you do.

> *"Blessed shall be your basket and your kneading bowl" (Deuteronomy 28:5).*

> *"And you shall remember the LORD your God, for it is He who gives you power to get wealth, that He may establish His covenant which He swore to your fathers, as it is this day" (Deuteronomy 8:18).*

> *"Thus says the LORD, your Redeemer, The Holy One of Israel: 'I am the LORD your God, Who teaches you to profit, Who leads you by the way you should go'" (Isaiah 48:17).*

Chapter 2

GOD MEANT IT AND I BELIEVE IT

There are Bible passages in reference to the subject of finance that some Christians do not understand. Let me share with you some of the hard to chew scriptures (and there are many more).

Hard To Chew Scriptures

.".. You shall lend to many nations, but you shall not borrow. And the Lord will make you the head and not the tail; you shall be above ONLY, and not be beneath ..." (Deuteronomy 28:12-13).

"Therefore do not worry, saying, 'What shall we eat?' or 'What shall we drink?' or 'What shall we wear?' For after all these things the Gentiles seek. For your heavenly Father knows that you need all these things. But seek first the kingdom of God and His righteousness, and ALL THESE THINGS SHALL BE ADDED TO YOU" (Matthew 6:31-33, Emphasis Mine).

> *"For you know the grace of our Lord Jesus Christ, that though He was rich, yet for your sakes He became poor, THAT YOU THROUGH HIS POVERTY MIGHT BECOME RICH"* (2 Corinthians 8:9).

I know what you may be thinking. You may be thinking that some of those promises are conditional. Yes, the first two are conditional. The question remains, 'Why are the righteous very poor?' Is there a judgement on us such that we are experiencing lack for not seeking God's Kingdom well enough? Even the Corinthians were told that Jesus became poor (though He was rich), so that they might become rich. Did they become wealthy? If this scripture is relevant to us, are we rich, individually and corporately? 'No,' would be my answer to the two.

It is shocking to see that a tiny fraction of professing Christians have this experience of abundant living. I am convinced that this fraction does not represent the fair proportion of the obedient. Again, there are many sincere seekers that died without this promises becoming a real experience before they did.

These are passages most Christians do not understand and I am sure you can now see why they have become difficult for some Christians to follow. I therefore came up with four reasons why we lack the understanding we so eagerly desire.

1. They are either not supposed to be in the Bible; or

2. We misunderstand and misapply them; or

3. There is something hindering their fulfilment and our enjoyment of them; or

4. Their fulfilment is for a future generation.

Of the four, I have chosen one which has formed the basis for writing this book. It also informed the subtitle to the book: 'Discover The Hidden Secrets Of The Affluent.'

First, we need to understand that God's plan of material blessing is not generational, dispensational, or sectarian. Secondly, no Earthly force is strong enough to hinder the fulfilment of God's promises and the flow of material blessings over an individual and certainly not over God's chosen people. Thirdly, "all Scripture is given by inspiration of God" (2 Timothy 3:16). The Bible passages and promises on God's will to prosper His children are valid, intentional and not accidental.

I believe with all my heart that God meant every word He said in the scriptures about financial prosperity. We therefore need to attempt to understand these Bible passages so we can correctly apply them, and they can become reality in our experiences. Jesus was not poor, and He wants you to be rich if you want to. Poverty is a choice.

Chapter 3

| POVERTY IS A CHOICE |

Poverty is a choice. Since God did not force salvation on you, which happens to be His greater desire, He will not force you to be rich. You may be born into poverty, but you are not created to be poor and you do not have to die a pauper. I have seen people picked themselves up from unthinkable depth of lack and rose to become the most successful people of our time. Walk with me and I will show you how.

Let me first show you a glimpse of the erroneous teachings about kingdom wealth. On one side of the spectrum are those that believe that every Christian should be rich and that if you are not rich, then there is something wrong with you. On the other side of the spectrum exists those that say that poverty is synonymous to piety.

None is true. You can be rich and not be holy, but you can also be holy and be rich at the same time. Let me explain. Job, Abraham, Isaac, and Jacob were rich and at the same time holy. Yes, they had their issues and sinned, yet God did not condemn them and certainly did not condone their actions. He remained associated with them despite their shortcomings. Most people have been taught that if you truly want to be holy, you have to renounce to be rich. Meaning that, you cannot be rich and remain holy. Well, that is a possibility but it is not a Bible teaching. It is humanistic teaching.

Didn't Jesus say to the rich young ruler in Matthew 19:21 to "go, sell what you have and give to the poor, and you will have treasure in heaven; and come, follow Me?"

Yes, He did, but he was not asking him to become poor. Let us observe it more closely.

First, the rich young ruler as he is described was a religious person but not a believer. He wanted to become "perfect." That was his initial quest. He asked in verse 17, "Good Teacher, what good thing shall I do that I may have eternal life?" Jesus answered, "Take up the cross, and follow Me." So, the rich young ruler was not a Christian.

The next thing is this. Jesus was teaching the rich young ruler to focus on heaven and not be arrogant; love God by loving His creation; and be generous in his giving. This teaching was clarified in Paul's letter to Timothy, his protégé.

> "Command those who are rich in this present age not to be haughty, nor to trust in uncertain riches but in the living God, who gives us richly all things to enjoy. Let them do good, that they be rich in good works, ready to give, willing to share, storing up for themselves a good foundation for the time to come, that they may lay hold on eternal life" (1 Timothy 6:17-19).

Apostle Paul said that rich people should be 'ready to give' and 'willing to share.' Like Jesus; Paul was not asking the rich to become poor and become like the people he was asking them to help.

The third point is that Jesus cares for the poor enough to raise their standards. He does not want the poor to stay poor. That was why he commanded that the rich man's focus should be to help the poor and not hoard; to be heavenly minded and be of earthly benefit. There is no point in making someone else poor if, in the first place, Jesus was trying to help other poor people.

Here is another common argument, "For you have the poor with you always." The verse is found in Mark 4:3-9.

> *"And being in Bethany at the house of Simon the leper, as He sat at the table, a woman came having an alabaster flask of very costly oil of spikenard. Then she broke the flask and poured it on His head. But there were some who were indignant among themselves, and said, "Why was this fragrant oil wasted? For it might have been sold for more than three hundred denarii and given to the poor." And they criticised her sharply. But Jesus said, "Let her alone. Why do you trouble her? She has done a good work for Me. For you have the poor with you always, and whenever you wish you may do them good; but Me you do not have always. She has done what she could. She has come beforehand to anoint My body for burial. Assuredly, I say to you, wherever this gospel is preached in the whole world, what this woman has done will also be told as a memorial to her"* (Mark 14:3-9).

At first, you might think that Jesus was in many ways contradicting His own teaching. Not at all. When you read that Jesus did not support the disciples but defended the woman, it must really seem confusing. To say, 'whenever you wish you may do them (the poor) good,' and to accord the woman a special tribute whenever the gospel is proclaimed can be asking too much.

On a closer look at this passage and others in the Bible relating to the same story, you will discover that, to the contrary, Jesus cared about the poor. He was just trying to address the motives behind the advice to protect the precious anointing oil. Let's see just one of them.

> "But one of His disciples, Judas Iscariot, Simon's son, who would betray Him, said, "Why was this fragrant oil not sold for three hundred denarii and given to the poor?" This he said, not that he cared for the poor, but because he was a thief, and had the money box; and he used to take what was put in it. But Jesus said, "Let her alone; she has kept this for the day of My burial. For the poor you have with you always, but Me you do not have always" (John 12:4-8).

If Jesus allowed the oil to be saved and sold later, little or none of the profit would have been transferred to the poor. Judas would have had a feasting at the expense of the needy. In fact, Judas was so condescending that he accepted thirty denarii in order to betray his own rabbi, which was a fraction and a tenth of the value of the oil.

> "Then one of the twelve, called Judas Iscariot, went to the chief priests and said, "What are you willing to give me if I deliver Him to you?" And they counted out to him thirty pieces of silver. So from that time he sought opportunity to betray Him" (Matthew 26:14-16).

To affirm His concern and care for the poor, Jesus commanded that any feasting must take into account their needs. There must be a fair allocation and adequate provisions for their needs.

> *"Then He also said to him who invited Him, "When you give a dinner or a supper, do not ask your friends, your brothers, your relatives, nor rich neighbours, lest they also invite you back, and you be repaid. But when you give a feast, invite the poor, the maimed, the lame, the blind. And you will be blessed, because they cannot repay you; for you shall be repaid at the resurrection of the just" (Luke 14:12-14).*

This profound teaching motivated Zacchaeus 'a sinner,' to refund four times whatever amount he took from other people, and to give half of his fortune to the poor.

> *"Then Zacchaeus stood and said to the Lord, "Look, Lord, I give half of my goods to the poor; and if I have taken anything from anyone by false accusation, I restore fourfold" (Luke 19:8).*

As can be seen from the pages of the four Gospels, Jesus' concern and care for the poor and needy is undeniable. But He never encouraged them to stay that way. "For you have the poor with you always" does not mean you are to become like them. What Jesus said to the disciples was that, the poor would always come around them, not that they would become poor.

It is not my intention to continue to refute the teachings of some who want you to take the oath of poverty whilst they remain comfortable. Some are even rich. It certainly is outside the scope of this writing. I have answered a lot of them in my soon-to-be-released book on biblical economics titled: "Jesus was not poor: He is rich and making people rich." I would rather focus my efforts at showing you how you can make that transition to riches if you choose to. Remember, poverty is a choice.

If today your experience or condition reflects lack, there is a way out. Do not accept anything short of God's will for you.

Chapter 4

EXPOSING THE WORLD FINANCIAL SYSTEM

The world financial system is designed to enslave. It is organised in such a way that if care is not taken, people will depend on it their entire life. When people borrow money, they become the slave of the lender. Let me expose you to how the world system works so that you can achieve financial freedom and be in charge of your life. I will share an example with you to illustrate this point.

In some parts of the world houses are built (not bought), but in a more civilised world most houses are bought on a scheme that is known as mortgages. Only few houses are built by individuals. However, this trend is slowly changing. When someone purchases a new property, there is always some sort of rejoicing. They might have taken a loan from a bank, or a financial institution technically referred to as a mortgage lender. The mortgagee is then referred to as a borrower. This borrowing according to the Bible makes the borrower a slave.

"Poor people are slaves of the rich. Borrow money and you are the lender's slave" (Proverbs 22:7, GNB).

In other words, anyone that takes a mortgage becomes a slave to the lender. As they work to pay off the money they owe, they are also working to make the lender a living. A man cannot continue to subscribe to this slavery system and suddenly expect to lend to nations. The good news is that, if you are in this system, you can change your circumstances by making sound financial choices and be free from the financial bondage.

In England, for example, a mortgage taken over twenty five years will grow to up to $2^{1/2}$ times payback. At the end of the mortgage term, the property will be worth close to 6 times the loan taken. (If there is no major crash in the property market, house prices double every 10 years). The lender's investment would have earned him 150% gain during this period and the borrower would have gained 86.4% in the process. If the home owner (the borrower) decides to sell the property and cash in his equity (or if the property is an investment property), the Government will draw a huge amount in Capital Gains Tax even though it did not contribute in any way to the loan.

Both the Government and the lender will get more than the property owner, and the sad reality is that the borrower does not own the property until the final due penny at redemption have been paid. That is why the Deed on the property comes to the property owner only after full redemption.

So what is my point here? If you took a 25-year mortgage, you would have spent an entire 15 years of your working life in an effort to pay off your mortgage, 9 of which are for the lender.

If you are a home owner I am not suggesting that you sell off your home, there is a positive side to this. Notice that you did not have to pay for the house in one lump sum. Well, you probably really didn't have that much. The lender took a risk on you hoping that you will keep on paying for the life of the loan. At least it was less risk to you. The rule of fairness says that the lender deserves a return on his investment.

The good news is this – after twenty five years of 'slavery', the borrower is now sitting on created wealth. Twenty five years is half the time a slave would have served a Jewish master. In the Old Testament, God instructed His people to free slaves after forty-nine (seven times seven) years – to liberate the slaves and all that belonged to them. It was done so no one would be enslaved for life. This is also why God instructed the Jews not to charge usury on loans. No high interest so people can enjoy living. (The Muslims still run this as part of Shariáh observations).

This slavery system also applies to other loans like car loan, student loan, and personal loans. While some people may not be able to afford to go on holidays because of the burden of debt and indebtedness, the 'city boys' (as they are called) under their employers receive between 40%-100% bonuses each year, and millions of pounds pay-offs end up in the hands of resigning directors.

Let us try to understand how the system operates from the life of Jacob in the Bible.

"When the boys grew up, Esau became a skillful hunter, a man of the field, but Jacob was a peaceful man (plain man, KJV), living in tents. Now Isaac loved Esau, because he had a taste for game, but Rebekah loved Jacob. When Jacob had cooked stew, Esau came in from the field and he was famished; and Esau said to Jacob, "Please let me have a swallow of that red stuff there, for I am famished." Therefore his

name was called Edom. But Jacob said, "First sell me your birthright." Esau said, "Behold, I am about to die; so of what {use} then is the birthright to me?" And Jacob said, "First swear to me"; so he swore to him, and sold his birthright to Jacob. Then Jacob gave Esau bread and lentil stew; and he ate and drank, and rose and went on his way. Thus Esau despised his birthright" (Genesis 25:27-34, NASB).

Exploitation

The world system is based on taking advantage of people in their time of need. It is a system of exploitation. It targets those who cannot control their appetites. It preys on people's weaknesses and hunger. This is expressed in Genesis 25 verse 29:

"…, he was weary"

."., he was hungry" (GNB, CEV).

"…, he was faint" (KJV)

When a person has a strong craving for something, the devil might use that against him. When there is a burning or desperate longing for something, someone will come in with an irresistible offer? Always. Sometimes we misinterpret this to be divine assistance whereas it might not be.

Not long ago a very close friend needed to raise some money, and I became burdened to help him. To my utter amazement the following day, I got two separate prearranged and approved credit offers from the same bank, one through the post and the other was a cold call. Now, it is reasonable and perhaps spiritual to conclude that was God. No, it's not that simple. Why did I say that? God instructed me not to accept any of the offers. I was quite disappointed since I felt I wouldn't be able to help my friend. The obligation to help my friend overwhelmed me to the point I started hurting.

I could easily have become another slave. I was hungry, and I became a target. The system was after me, but I escaped its net not because I was smart but because God saved me. A weak person can be an easy target for the predators.

At the time of writing this book, Britain is a trillion and a third pounds into debt, yet getting credit is easier compared to just a few years ago.

My very first application for a credit card was to American Express, but my application was turned down. That was over 16 years ago. However, between then and now, I have turned down 3 of their special offers.

Haste And Impatience

The purposes of God often develop slowly because His grand designs are never hurried. The great New England preacher, Phillips Brooks, was noted for his poise and calm manner. At times, he suffered moments of frustration and irritability. One day a friend saw him feverishly pacing the floor like a caged lion. "What's the problem, Mr. Brooks?" he asked.

"The trouble is that I'm in a hurry, but God isn't!

Haven't we felt the same way many times?

Some of the greatest missionaries of history devotedly spread the seed of God's Word. They had to wait long periods before seeing the fruit of their efforts. William Carey, for example, laboured seven years before the first Hindu convert was brought to Christ in Burma. Adoniram Judson toiled seven years before his faithful preaching was rewarded. In Western Africa, it was 14 years before one convert was received into the Christian Church. In New Zealand, it took nine years, and in Tahiti, it was 16 years before the first harvest of souls began.

Thomas A Kempis described that kind of patience in these words, "He deserves not the name 'patient' who is only willing to suffer as much as he thinks proper, and for whom he pleases. The truly patient man asks nothing from whom he suffers, whether his superior, his equal, or his subordinate. But from whomever, or how much, or how often wrong is done to him, he accepts it all as from the hand of God and counts it gain!"i

From our main story, Esau's problem was not just hunger. Being hungry is not necessarily bad. Hunger is a sign that the digestive system is fully functional. Everyone will get hungry at a stage. But if a person does not eat for a length of time, he will die.

Esau's first mistake was to fall prey to a system waiting to pounce on him. He allowed his appetite to get out of control and traded-in his future. His second mistake was that he was impatient. Making decisions when vulnerable is unwise. The world system has a way of finding out people's financial weaknesses, and will usually offer a quick getaway, making it easier for people to get into more debt. It's a system of slavery. It knows people would like a quick way out. It always has a readymade answer. The only time credit is never available is when someone has had a bad credit or no traceable credit scoring. Bad credit is usually a result of being financially squeezed and drained until the person can no longer bleed.

Though Esau caught game and somehow dragged it home, he could not wait to cook it. He was too impatient to roast his game. Of course, it would have taken some time to prepare the cooked food. He therefore went for a ready-to-eat meal. The Bible describes this as laziness.

> *"The lazy man does not roast what he took in hunting,*
> *but diligence is a man's precious possession"*
> *(Proverbs 12:27, NASB).*

The world financial system not only preys on your hunger, it does on your impatience too. It says you can have it now because if you wait, you may not find it anymore, or prices will go up. Sometimes a prey can get an offer of up to 5 years interest free credit in addition. And we often fail to read the small prints.

Advertisement

The world system also uses promotion to win over its targets. It is amazing to see well known multinational companies spending thousands of pounds on twenty-second advertisements. They use expensive and sensual images to market their products and services. They use words that we would remember until the ad pops up the next time. They form impressions on our minds that stay with us. They use slogans like "every little helps" or "it's good to talk", phrases that haunt us wherever we go. Each time we hear the words, we become sorry for not having the product. When we finally do, we feel like we belong to an elite group.

Designer trainers, suits, shoes, caps, watches, smart phones and more. We often think they are the best, but that is not necessarily true; it's the power of imagery and sound.

Esau said to Jacob "Please feed me with that same red stew." Two things struck me in this verse: the red colour of the stew and the word "same."

Colourful adverts can have a great impact on hungry people. What caught Esau's attention first and foremost was the red colour. Perhaps Esau would have ignored his appetite until such time that he had his own red stew prepared if it were not the richness of the stew. However, the red colouration was overwhelming. There is something very passionate and special about red.

Red is the lowest of the seven colours in the visible spectrum and is known as a "warm" colour. It is stimulating and energising, so it is helpful for tiredness and lethargy, to stimulate low blood pressure, to boost sluggish circulation. Red should not be used on anyone with hypertension (raised blood pressure) or as a colour treatment since this colour increases blood flow.

Red, in its most positive sense, is the colour for courage, strength and pioneering spirit. The red energy is the slowest vibration of the rainbow energies. Red is the grounding colour. It is what gives us our vitality, and passion for being on the physical plane. The power of red can be the power of emotion, finance, or power in relationships. Red is symbolic of a strong willed person. It can relate to pain on the physical or pain in the emotions that are so strong it is felt in the physical.

Using colours well in the home is a way of creating a balanced environment. Red is energising and excites the emotions, and can stimulate the appetite. It is often used in restaurants. It can be used in any activity area, but red needs careful choice of character and depth and the space in which it is to be used as it can make a space look smaller and can be claustrophobic or oppressive. However, used well, red and its variations can make a space feel warm and cosy.

In the most damaging aspect, it is the colour of anger, violence and brutality and, interestingly, before World War II, it was noted that a lot of red was being worn. Red provides energy to excitement and with impatience it can cause frustration. Following feelings of anger and frustration we can often feel depleted of energy. When we are angry and frustrated we see 'red.' It relates to survival issues and the life force. It stands for power: our own, others and the power struggles that can sometimes occur between the two. This is the colour of being in the physical and the need for material possession.

If a person sacrifices oneself for others, he may become physically vulnerable. Red relates to the physical in all its aspects and often it can show that the person is not satisfied with the surrounding physical environment, or even their own physical body. Red is the colour of blood, the heat of the temper, and also inflamed physical conditions. Then Christ's energy and sacrifice – that is its ultimate.

It is not surprising that Esau's means "Red Hair."

Be careful when you watch ads with too much red in it. It says "come and get me" and you'll fall into its trap. They are there to get your attention but don't fall for it.

"Do not look on the wine when it is RED, when it sparkles in the cup, when it swirls around smoothly; at the last it bites like a serpent, and stings like a viper. Your eyes will see strange things, and your heart will utter perverse things. Yes, you will be like one who lies down in the midst of the sea, or like one who lies at the top of the mast, saying: "they have struck me, but I was not hurt; they have beaten me, but I did not feel it. When shall I awake, that I may seek another drink?" (Proverbs 23:31-35).

There is nothing wrong in red stew, but not everything that glitters is gold. Had Esau waited to prepare his stew, he would not only have enjoyed it but enjoyed it in abundance and probably have left-overs. Waiting to enjoy may be better and long lasting. So do not buy into this idea of quick deals and special offers.

The other thing that caught my attention in the verse is the word "same." It is not impossible that there had been a dialogue earlier between the twin brothers. Jacob probably wanted Esau to have the other stew, but Esau would not be dissuaded otherwise. He wanted that same red stew and would not settle for any other. If you've had something before, it is very likely you would always prefer it to other things especially if it was the best at the first try. The devil may hammer on the same issue to score points on you. So beware!

Desperation

The world system targets those who are weak and feeble. It targets those who are impatient. Finally, it targets those who are desperate. It uses the media - TV, Internet, Radio and Print – to win over its targets. Perhaps gunning for those that are desperate and have lost hope is the most deadly of its dirty tactics.

Esau said to Jacob "I am about to die." Clearly, he was very famished but he was nowhere close to death. No one previously healthy has died from missing a day's meal.

On the contrary, research has proven that a healthy person can survive up to forty days just on water. David Blaine survived on water for over 40 days at London's Tower Bridge in September of 2003. We also have the biblical example of Moses, who went 80 days without food. Elijah the prophet and our Lord Jesus Christ also went 40 days each without food.

Though he was very hungry, Esau was not going to die. To palliate his desire, he pretended he was at the point of death. If it had been so, was it not better for him to die in honour than to live in shame; to die under a blessing than to live under a curse?

The adverts are made such that you would want what you do not need. It creates the thirst and makes the desire stronger. It tells you 'if you don't get it now you will die.'

The pain and discomfort you are currently experiencing will not lead to death. You did not die when you, your spouse and a friend were sharing a bed-sit in a bedroom apartment. Remember how you used to take turns to sleep. You were able to sleep in the night while your friend went to his night shift and vice versa when you were at work during the day. You didn't die.

You have moved up a little bit. Thank God. You now reside in a two bedroom house with your spouse and your two boys. You only need two bedrooms, but something inside you suddenly feels like you are getting choked in the two bedroom, and you want three or four bedroom house with two lounges, three baths, front and rear gardens and a large garage. And you want it now.

It may be true that the two bedroom is becoming too small. It may equally be that you cannot afford what you desire just yet. Waiting another year or two until you can afford a bigger house won't hurt, and you certainly won't die. In your mind, you are just replaying the property programmes you've exposed yourself to over a period of time.

That was exactly what happened to us when my wife joined me in England. I was sharing a one-bedroom flat with a friend. He worked night shifts, and we worked day shifts. That was how we survived until we were able to rent our own apartment. For the length of time we were sharing, things were difficult for all involved but none of us died. We are better off today. Praise be to God.

This is how the world system works. It is the job of the advertising agents to make a want become a need. Have you ever wondered why the product on offer is always the last copy, or they tell you the offer will soon end? So you think, "If I don't get it now, I may miss out or die."

I remember desiring a laptop and then visited a computer store. On arriving at the store, I discovered that the particular model and specifications that would meet my need was on an offer that was to end that evening.

Honestly, I felt I was going to miss out on the offer if I did not buy on the last day of the offer. It felt like an offer of "a lifetime." As I do not buy things on impulse, I decided I would wait until I had a good comparison and shopped around a bit even if it meant going without that particular offer. I went back the next day with an open mind to see if new offers have been released so I could start my shopping-around much early. To my utter amazement, the previous day's offer came back on a week's extension. It eventually turned out to be the best offer that was going at the time. I realised I did not miss out on the offer after all, although I was 'sort of' a day late.

Once, a gentleman walked into our office offering a competitive telephone service. We happened to be a desirable target because we just opened a business, and we needed a phone line. After we signed the agreement, we had a ten day cooling period which was statutory with another 30-day free trial period. "If you are no longer interested in the offer or got a better deal at any stage during this cooling period and the free month, you can cancel and switch to another service provider," added the Sales Agent. Unfortunately, many people forget the cooling period and the free month and lose the freedom to opt out.

Exactly two days later, someone walked in from the same company offering the same service for a 60-day free trial period. After I revealed to her that I had only just signed an agreement with the same company, she requested to know the agent. I told her the name, and she confirmed that the other person was her manager. Can you imagine? I had just signed a contract with a manager of a company less than three days ago when I could have waited to get a better deal signed with the junior staff. I thought I was going to miss out if I didn't do it there and then without knowing that the company was going to offer a better deal just days after.

Many people have gone into serious debt problems because they won't wait. They thought they would die without the goods or services they bought. They are now paying a bigger price with their lives.

Often, you would visit a store and buy items on offer and more often than not, there is the possibility that walking a few stores down the street, you would discover a far bigger and better offer. Then sometimes, if you had waited, you would have gotten a better offer from the same shop. As they close one offer, they release another offer better than the last. You would not find a shop releasing a new offer worse than the last. In order to keep their customers, stores usually will try to better their last offer.

The sad truth, worse than spending the money we don't have, is that, we underutilise the products we buy and were told would make us better people. Many of our modern gadgets are underutilised. We only use a few of the several buttons: play, pause, rewind and stop, no more. When they were first introduced, they cost a fortune, and we thought they would improve the way we live. The DVD player is a good example. Now they cost peanuts, and you can even get two for the price of one!

Those that did not get them when they arrived in the market finally did when the technologies behind them had fully evolved. If you buy any new equipment today, I guarantee they would be out of date in just six months. So it's not worth the rush and desperation.

Chapter 5

PROTECT YOURSELF FROM THE WORLD FINANCIAL SYSTEM

Do Not Shop Tired

Do not shop when you are physically tired. You might make poor judgements. The truth is that if you are tired, you will just want to get your shopping done with, and you cannot be bothered walking around any longer. This also is true when you are vulnerable and weak.

It may be better to take time off, go into a restaurant and cool down first. After you have had a bit of rest, you can resume your shopping. It may be better to make enquiries about the product before you start off from home, and adequate provision for breaks when you are shopping.

You may sometimes be physically healthy but mentally depleted. If you have tried on several occasions to get out of debt which has taken many years, you may become anxious and fearful the next time you hear the mail drop or a knocking on your door. This often results in psychological anguish and anxiety.

An average person's fear is focused on 40% things that will never happen; 30% things about the past that cannot be changed; 12% things about criticism by others, mostly untrue; 10% about health, which gets worse with stress; and 8% about real problems that will be faced.

The next time you receive a threat letter with a deadline, do not immediately reach out for the loan offer you recently received. You should first sit back and relax and see how you can negotiate with the creditors. They usually are willing to dialogue and discuss your options. Look at your options and carefully evaluate them. Do not rush into any conclusions which in the end may prove costly.

Do Not Rush Out

Plato wrote the first sentence of his famous Republic nine different ways before he was satisfied. Cicero practiced speaking before friends every day for thirty years to perfect his elocution. Noah Webster laboured 36 years writing his dictionary, crossing the Atlantic twice to gather material. Milton rose at 4am every day in order to have enough hours for his Paradise Lost. Gibbon spent 26 years on his Decline and Fall of the Roman Empire. Bryant rewrote one of his poetic masterpieces 99 times before publication, and it became a classic.

It was said that Thomas Edison performed 8,000 (sic) experiments before he succeeded in producing a storage battery. We might assume the famous inventor would have had some serious doubts along the way. When asked if he ever became discouraged working so long without results, Edison replied, "Results? Well, at least we know 8,000 things that do not work."

Wilma did not get much of a head start in life. A bout with polio left her left leg crooked, and her foot twisted inward, so she had to wear leg braces. After seven years of painful therapy, she could walk without her braces. At age 12, Wilma tried out for a girls' basketball team but did not make it. Determined, she practiced with a girl and two boys every day. The following year she made the team. When a college track coach saw her during a game, he talked her into letting him train her as a runner. By age 14, she had outrun the fastest sprinters in the U.S. In 1956 Wilma made the U.S. Olympic team, but showed poorly. That bitter disappointment motivated her to work harder for the 1960 Olympics in Rome, and there, Wilma Rudolph won three gold medals, the most a woman had ever won at the time.

People may not start in the same place, at the same time, or in the same way. Nevertheless, everyone will have their own shot at their own time. Some people start early in life and some late; some starts rough and others smooth. How you start will profoundly affect how you are likely to end, but more remarkable is being able to end well.

Esau woke up early in the morning, sharpened his weapons (or loaded his guns), and then into the field he went. Though hoping to kill 'game', he risked being killed. We noticed he got his game howbeit with struggles, fights and many failed trials.

Heavy or light, Esau carried his 'game' through the doors. Arriving home, he was now on level pegging with Jacob. What was Jacob's starting point was Esau's halfway position. He had the cooked meal at home even before Esau arrived with his 'game.' What Esau did with the raw meat, we would never know.

Though Jacob had a head start, Esau now had an opportunity to prove his worth. His originally plan was to come home with his game and have a sumptuous dinner made from his gain. Both Jacob and Esau had raw materials (raw meat).

Much red meat could have finally become delicious steak, but many people would give up their raw meat for someone's steak because they are not willing to persevere. It is sad how many people quit at the edge of their breakthrough; after all the effort. What a waste! Postage stamps are getting more expensive, but at least they have one attribute that most of us could emulate: they stick to one thing until they arrive at the intended destination.

On March 6, 1987, Eamon Coughlan, the Irish world record holder at 1500 meters, was running in a qualifying heat at the World Indoor Track Championships in Indianapolis. With two and a half laps left, he tripped. He fell, but he got up and with great effort managed to catch the leaders. With only twenty yards left in the race, he was in third place - good enough to qualify for the finals. He looked over his shoulder to the inside, and, seeing no one, he let up. But another runner, charging hard on the outside, passed Coughlan a yard before the finish, thus eliminating him from the finals. Coughlan's impressive comeback attempt was rendered meaningless by taking his eyes off the finish line. It is tempting to let up when the sights around us look favourable, but we end well in the Christian race only when we fix our eyes on the goal: Jesus Christ.

During the Vietnam War, the Texas Computer millionaire, H. Ross Perot decided he would give a Christmas present to every American prisoner of war in Vietnam. According to David Frost, who tells the story, Perot had thousands of packages wrapped and prepared for shipping. He chartered a fleet of Boeing 707s to deliver them to Hanoi, but the war was at its height, and the Hanoi government said it would refuse to cooperate. No goodwill was likely, officials explained, while American bombers were devastating Vietnamese villages. The wealthy Perot offered to hire an American construction firm to help rebuild what Americans had knocked down. The government still would not cooperate. Christmas drew near, and the packages were unsent. Refusing to give up, Perot finally took off in his chartered fleet and flew to Moscow, where his aides mailed the packages, one at a time, at the Moscow central post office. They were delivered intact.

You may have had a brilliant idea and started working on it but, as soon as you found an easy alternative, you took the shortcut instead of following through with your dream. You need patience and dedication. Esau was impatient and lazy.

> *"The lazy man does not roast what he took in hunting,*
> *but diligence is a man's precious possession"*
> *(Proverbs 12:27).*

Do Not Buy On Impulse, Plan Ahead

Envisage your need. Plan ahead. Pre-empt the future and plan for it. Do not buy things when you are desperately in need of them. Do not wait until the last minute. Anticipate, envisage, and predict what you might need at least in the near future. If you do not, you will be under pressure to buy NOW. Plan for it, and save up for it. This is the attitude of a champion.

Always remember this: procrastination is dangerous and leads to inevitable consequences. Today was yesterday's tomorrow and tomorrow will in a moment become today, and today will become yesterday. Do not allow any distractions; no matter how convincing they may seem. If you want to live a better tomorrow, prepare for it today. Nothing just happens. You can save yourself heartache if you attend to things without delay.

An incident from the American Revolution illustrates what tragedy can result from procrastination. It was reported that Colonel Johann Rahl, commander of the British troops in Trenton, New Jersey, was playing cards when a courier brought an urgent message stating that General George Washington was crossing the Delaware River. Rahl put the letter in his pocket and did not bother to read it until the game ended. Then, realising the seriousness of the situation, he hurriedly tried to rally his men to meet the coming attack, but his procrastination was his undoing. He and many of his men were killed, and the rest of the regiment were captured.

Nolbert Quayle comments: "Only a few minutes' delay cost him his life, his honour, and the independence of his soldiers. Earth's history is strewn with the wrecks of half-finished plans and unexecuted resolutions. 'Tomorrow' is the excuse of the lazy and refuge of the incompetent."

Time waits for no one, plan now. One of the reasons a woman does not deliver her baby the same time she conceives is so she can prepare. Just imagine waiting until close to her third trimester before she starts shopping for baby things. She would be overwhelmed by the sheer volume of what needs to be done, and she is also likely to buy the wrong things.

Many years ago, we decided we were going to move to a bigger accommodation which also happened to be newly built. From one bedroom to three bedrooms; we knew without a doubt that we were going to need a lot more furniture, bedding, and so on. We then made a plan to start buying everything we would need a year in advance. Most of them were purchased at discounted 'sale' prices since we had time to shop around. The only old pieces of items we took with us into the new house were; a year old shelf-freezer and a six-month old washing machine. Every other thing was new.

Esau did not plan ahead. He should have envisaged that his raw meat was not going to meet his urgent need. He then should have prepared a snack that would have kept him going until he roasted his game. He could easily have plucked fruits on his way home. Esau was 'short-sighted' in a sense.

> *"Because of laziness, the building decays, and through idleness of hands, the house leaks"* *(Ecclesiastes 10:18).*

> *"When no work is done, the roof goes in, and when the hands do nothing, water comes into the house"* *(Ecclesiastes 10:18, BBE).*

Do Not Sell Out

Jacob said to Esau "sell your birthright as of this day." Esau did not advertise his birthright, he only wanted red stew.

The world is trying to buy you out. It is bent on enslaving you and buying your future. Do not sell your future. Each time you buy something, an exchange takes place. When you buy with cash, you are exchanging your right to the cash. It is no longer yours. You lose the right to the money. The income you receive is a payback for the time you spent, and the time you spent is your life. Life is measured in time and time is rewarded in cash. Money is a reward for your time. When you buy with cash (not borrowed cash), you are exchanging your past, but when you buy with credit or loan, you are exchanging or selling your future.

Don't Be Pressured

Many sales agents have a target to achieve and are paid on commission. That is what most live on. Therefore, they would try every possible way to get you to sign above the dotted line. Jacob said to Esau "sell your birthright as of this day." It simply means "sell your future, now." Does that sound familiar? Buy now, pay later. The sales agents will often say they are in your area only on the day.

I met one agent at a local supermarket desperately trying to get me to change my electricity and gas supplier to the firm she represented. She told me they were only there for that day, but I knew we were going to meet again, though at the time, it was only an educated guess. As it happened, I did not return to the supermarket that week but met her at another shopping mall where we had rented a business unit. She immediately recognised me as I walked towards her, and we have since become acquaintances.

In another instance, at a shopping mall close to where we live, I found a 'Buy one, get one free' offer on cooked ham. If you have children of school age, you would just jump at the offer because it means you can save on sandwich fillings. Many people grabbed the offer and left, but I passed on the deal. Why? The ham was going to expire in just three days. It meant the people that bought it must eat it within three days. I can just imagine them chucking most of it inside the rubbish bin or eating cooked ham for breakfast, lunch, and dinner for the next three days. Perhaps they did not need it; they just did not want to miss out on the deal. It is called FOMO (FEAR OF MISSING OUT).

I have made it a practice not to make decisions on impulse unless there is urgency to it. My philosophy is, "if it cannot wait, it can wait." I have developed the word deal to a 'D.E.A.L.' acronym which translates 'DON'T EMBRACE ANY LIES.'

Chapter 6

| SOFT AND HARD LOANS |

Soft Loans

The rule of thumb is, 'do not loan if you can avoid not to.' However, if you are finding it hard not to borrow, the following might help you in making that decision.

Consider soft loans

There are a few tips I would like to share with you on soft loans.

• If you are a student, Student Loans are better than bank loans. The good thing about this facility is that you do not pay anything until you start working. Even when you start working, you will not have to pay until you reach certain income threshold, and when you start paying, it is usually in proportion to your earning. Also, low interest is charged on Students Loans compared to banks. Finally, as a surety, the scheme is regulated and managed by the government.

• Secondly, consider borrowing from close friends or members of your immediate family (i.e. father, mother or sibling, no more). At times, it may be better to borrow from the bank than to borrow from a family member. This is because your relationship will be affected if you cannot pay back the loan. However, if you know they can handle any delay, it is better to loan from them. At least, it is interest free, and there would be minimal or flexible repayment term. Integrity says you need to fulfil your part of the contract and pay them back on schedule.

• Thirdly, go for '0% interest until…' Notice, I did not say 'No payment until…' There is a difference between the two: the first means you will be paying 0% interest for a certain period while the second means you may wish to pay nothing until a certain period. It is clear, 0% interest means you have to be making regular payments with the hope that you will fully discharge the loan at the end of its term. If you do not pay the minimum at the end of the month, you will be entered a missed payment which may result in a default. You can also accrue late payment charges though the offer is interest free. Though they allow you to spread the payments, you may not realise that you will get defaults and have to pay penalties on missed payments. Interest is calculated from the time you took the loan if you do not fully discharge the loan during the interest free period.

However, 'Pay nothing until…' means there are no penalties if you decide not to pay anything until closer to its redemption. You still need to be careful of missed or late payments and defaults. No interest will be paid if the loan is fully redeemed at the end of the period. But if you do not fully discharge the loan at the agreed time, interest will be recalculated from the time the loan was taken.

If you already used your credit facilities before taking advantage of another '0% interest…' offer or 'pay nothing until…' offer, ensure that payments made are properly allocated or posted toward the right offer. You may need to make a phone call to the company giving such instruction. If you do not, the payment may be allocated to the wrong offer; you will get a missed payment, a late payment fee and a default.

Here is a note of caution. Do not accept the offer of deferred payments if there is no absolute guarantee you are going to be able to pay back at the end of the agreed period. This is what I mean by absolute guarantee: if your circumstance is not going to improve during the period of the offer, do not accept the offer. You will just be accumulating debt. If you cannot afford it now, what is the possibility you will be able to afford it in six months except your financial situation changes for the better?

Without this absolute guarantee, I prefer to be on the side of caution. If you cannot afford it now, you may not even be able to afford it in six months except your situation changes or you create a new stream of income.

The Truth about Credit Cards

• Use your Savings. If you set aside any amount of money in any savings account for future spending and you suddenly have an emergency, it is wise to take part of the savings to cater for the crisis than use the credit cards straightaway. However, most credit cards offer up to 59 days free credit on card purchases. If you pounce on your credit card, you will have to clear the credit in about 59 days. Whereas, if you first use the savings for emergency, and later use the credit card for the future spending, it buys you more time to address the emergency.

- Avoid using credit card cheque or making cash withdrawals from your credit cards. When you withdraw money or use a credit card Cheque, you would be asked to pay a percentage of the money taken or an administration fee and a higher interest rate which is also calculated from the transaction date, but if you use the card in the store, no administrative fee would be charged, you pay lower interest rate and have 59 days to pay back without any interest. If you cannot pay back what is expected at the end of the month, try always to pay above the minimum.

- Some credit card companies will allocate payments to clear lower interest first though it was taken last. For example if you took two separate loans with the first having a higher interest than the second, when you pay back, part of the loan payment would be allocated to the second transaction instead of the first. The repayment should have been allocated in the order the money was taken. Demand that the money should be properly allocated.

- Different rates apply to different withdrawals. You usually pay higher interest on cash withdrawals.

Hard Loans

Secondly, consider hard loans. Whatever happens, do not take any Hire Purchases please! It is also called closed-end leasing or rent to own. The so-called buyer who has the use of the goods is not the legal owner during the term of the hire-purchase contract. If the buyer defaults in paying the instalments, the owner may repossess the goods.

- Talking about Bank loans: shop around for the lowest interest. There are over 51,000 financial institutions in the United Kingdom all looking for your money. Except your credit score is adverse, you can be picky. I remember giving a beggar 50p, and he asked whether I could increase it to £1, but I refused. Even beggars sometimes choose. So shop around; there is no harm in asking. The worst response you can get is a 'no.' If you are offered a loan, avoid securing the loan on your property. If you struggle to pay back the loan, they will come after your house. If you do not have job security, take a payment protection with your loan. It means you will be paying more, but at least the lender will pay if or when you cannot pay. If it is a small loan, you may avoid payment protection. The law in the UK now demands that the loan and the payment protection insurance should be two separate contracts.

- Releasing equity on mortgages. Loans raised by releasing the equity on a mortgage are usually secured on the mortgage. Again, be wise. This will increase your monthly repayments. If you cannot pay back the loan, your home will be at risk. The advantage of this form of lending is that you might get the same interest rate if the advance is taken at the same time you re-mortgage the property. Even when you release the equity on your property, never take more than 20% equity. As an example, Capital Gains Tax belongs to the government when the property is sold – assuming it is your investment property. If you take 100% equity, you will need another loan to cover the shortfall when you sell so you can pay the government Capital Gains Tax. This may be different from one country to another. The point here is this; do not use any equity if you can avoid it.

Downsize

Consider downsizing. What does that mean? It means cut down. In layman's terms, it means selling anything valuable so as to raise required funds. It may mean selling the big cars to get a small car. It may be moving from a detached house to a semi-detached house. It may be reducing the number of dinning out and holidays. It may be wearing the same clothes and shoes for longer. These can be done with purposeful determination. It may take a summer or two, or surprisingly less. The pain will disappear shortly after you have recovered.

> *"...After you have suffered a little while, he will restore, support, and strengthen you, and he will place you on a firm foundation" (I Peter 5:10, NLT).*

Chapter 7

| STEPS TO DEBT CANCELLATION |

et me take you back to the introduction of this book. I shared the story of a widow who was to lose everything in her future because she lacked divine inspiration. Let me now walk you through, a verse at a time, what she did on her journey from poverty to prosperity. In six steps, the widow went from rag to riches.

1. Search Your House

> "So Elisha said to her, "What shall I do for you? Tell me, what do you have in the house?" And she said, "Your maidservant has nothing in the house but a jar of oil" (2 Kings 4:2).

The prophet's wife was going to lose everything she had, yet her miracle was in the same house. It was not in a conference or convention. It was not in an anointing service or a miracle service somewhere in the city. Her miracle was in her house. Take a careful look at the situations described below.

- The weapon that broke down a world super power and paved the way for a nation to be set free was just a stick in the hands of Moses.

- While Esau went to the wilderness to struggle for a game, Jacob just took an animal from the garden, killed it and roasted it for his dying father and in the process got the blessing. He did not have to leave the house or risk his life.

- The weapon that brought down a mighty man of war, the Philistine Goliath was just a sling in the hands of David.

- The cake and oil that was to sustain the Widow of Zarephath was in her house; yet, she was going to die of hunger.

- The meal that fed 5,000 men was in the hands of a small boy in the village camp, not in the city.

Right on the inside of you lie all that you need to make it in life. There is something you must be good at. Maybe you can sing. Maybe you like to teach. Some people can talk. Sometimes what you need to breakthrough is not new ideas but the abandoned ones. John the Baptist's office, was in the wilderness, yet men left the city to draw from him. If you possess something that would benefit the world, you will be sought after.

This is the crux of this book. The emphasis is on the kneading bowl; what you can do with your hands. We use the kneading bowl to make the dough when baking. The good thing about the kneading bowl is that it is unlimited in its use.

2. Be Open And Honest About Your Situation

"So Elisha said to her, "What shall I do for you? Tell me, what do you have in the house?" And she said, "Your maidservant has nothing in the house but a jar of oil" (2 Kings 4:2).

You cannot go around telling everybody what you are going through, but there are certain people that should know. Many of us are confused on the difference between positive faith confession and negative doubt confession. You can tell some people 'it is well', but not an 'Elijah' or an 'Elisha,' the 'prophets' of your life.

Reading the story that followed (2 Kings 4:8-37), we noticed also that the only son of the Shunammite woman died. So the mother went after the man of God, Prophet Elisha. On her way down, her husband asked what the problem was, and she replied "it is well." As she was approaching the prophet's estate, Gehazi (the prophet-in-training) asked the reason for her visit. She again replied, "It is well." However, when the Shunammite woman got to Elisha, she did not say it is well. She opened up her heart and complained bitterly.

While you have to be careful about who knows your story, you need to be discerning, so you don't miss the person God has sent to help you. When I ask people about their life and circumstances, and they tell me it is well, I take it that it is well. I am not interested in gathering information. What would I even do with it? However, if they choose to tell me, I can pray with them or encourage them with a word from Scripture or I may know someone who can help.

The widow (the prophet's wife) could have said to Elisha that all is well and her two son could have been taken as slaves. Instead, she said, "Your maidservant has nothing in the house but a jar of oil." It means, "I have no future, but I have hope."

3. Be Ready To Do Whatever God Instructs

"Then he said, "Go, borrow vessels from everywhere, from all your neighbours – empty vessels; do not gather just a few" (2 Kings 4:3).

Borrow, empty vessels, from neighbours? Yes, more borrowing, empty vessels, from neighbours. Ridicule upon ridicule? No, it was not ridicule, it was a miracle. This is not something I would advocate, but it was what the prophet said. You don't go for a loan consolidation. It's never going to work unless God ask you to.

God may occasionally ask you to do something unusual and unconventional. What God instructs doesn't have to make sense. Like bringing down the wall by shouting and singing praises to God. Like facing a super power with just a stick. Like killing a soldier with the sling and a stone. Like serving water to guests which on the way, turned to wine. Like throwing a stick into the water, to make a sunken metal axe float. When God instructs, it doesn't have to make sense. Yet, if you obey, you will benefit. You just have to be sure you heard God clearly.

4. Enlarge Your Vision

"Then he said, "Go, borrow vessels from everywhere, from all your neighbours — empty vessels; do not gather just a few. 6 Now it came to pass, when the vessels were full, that she said to her son, "Bring me another vessel." And he said to her, "There is not another vessel." So the oil ceased" (2 Kings 4:3 & 6).

Elisha said to her, don't think too little; think big. He said, "don't gather just a few." Some of us think too little. Some of us Christians are too modest; we aim so low. Can I challenge you to aim higher, reach higher, go larger?

Don't be afraid of an increase. Jabez was in many ways better than his brothers but demanded more from God. God is not embarrassed when you ask for more. He has the resources.

"Now Jabez was more honourable than his brothers, and his mother called his name Jabez, saying, "Because I bore him in pain." And Jabez called on the God of Israel saying, "Oh, that You would bless me indeed, and enlarge my territory, that Your hand would be with me, and that You would keep me from evil, that I may not cause pain!" So God granted him what he requested" (2 Chronicles 4:9-10).

"Now to Him who is able to do exceedingly abundantly above all that we ask or think, according to the power that works in us" (Ephesians 3:20).

As long as the family found more vessels, the oil continued to run. When there was not another vessel, the oil ceased. You are the only one that can limit your scope.

5. Protect Your Idea, Shut The Door

Go behind closed doors. Your idea is your intellectual property; trademark it, copyright it, insure it, and protect it.

> *"And when you have come in, you shall shut the door behind you and your sons; then pour it into all those vessels, and set aside the full ones." So she went from him and shut the door behind her and her sons, who brought the vessels to her; and she poured it out"* (2 Kings 4:4-5).

Have you noticed that immediately you have an idea and you share it with certain people; it will just die a premature death and never take off. There are too many sniffer dogs around. They do not like you. They want to steal your business ideas. They may even discourage you and try to talk you out of doing it. They are called dream killers. Choose carefully whom you share your dreams with. Some people don't wish you well. A typical example is Joseph. Hearing his dreams, his brothers betrayed him.

6. Make Profit

> *"Then she came and told the man of God. And he said, "Go, sell the oil and pay your debt; and you and your sons live on the rest"* (2 Kings 4:7).

Sorted, she is now debt free. This is your opportunity to be financially independent. Now, you can start. You can put your finance back together. God can fulfil this desire of your heart.

A lot of people want to pray to God to cancel their debts, but all God does sometimes is to give them an idea, a word, an inspiration and they cancel their own debt. God will help you to profit so you can pay off your debt.

Next chapter, I will discuss the issue of profit making.

Chapter 8

HOW TO SECURE YOUR ECONOMIC FUTURE

There Is Something In Your Garden

Millions of people are looking for things outside their boundaries; whereas all they need is to look in their houses or in their gardens. Many like Esau wake up early, risk their lives, chasing after what they already have at home. They then return to eat what they left behind. What's the point in all that? Chasing after the wind!

Jacob and Esau lived in the same house. Whatever Jacob put together to prepare the stew was already in the house. We are nowhere told that he went after any ingredient, but Esau went to look for what was already in the house.

It is fair to say that Jacob's miracle was in his garden. Yours may be your natural aptitude or ability. It may be a staff like that of Moses or a sling like that of David. It may be the jar of oil or a little boy's lunch. Everybody has something in the garden waiting to be used to make life better for them.

Nineteenth Century inventor Gail Borden was obsessed with the idea of condensing food. His first attempt, a condensed "meat biscuit," failed miserably. But an ocean voyage gave birth to a better idea. Borden was concerned about the sickly condition of the children on board. Cows on the ship were too seasick to produce healthy milk, and four children died from drinking contaminated milk. Borden was determined to condense milk so that it would be safe and easily transported. After many tries, he devised a vacuum system that removed water from milk. Conditions during the Civil War made the canned milk a success, and Borden made a fortune. His epitaph, inscribed on a grave the shape of a milk can, was, "I tried and failed; I tried again and again, and succeeded."

Cook Something

The other problem with many people is that they refuse to cook because they lack the knowledge or the creativity to do so. Like Esau, they have the raw materials but do nothing with them.

What happened to Esau's game? Did he finally cook it? Did he throw it away? Was it taken from him by Jacob's trickery? My guess is that he did nothing with it worth recording. He probably wasted it. The problem with a lot of people is that they cannot be bothered to 'cook.' That is the difference between a consumer and a producer. The producer cooks and the consumer eats. So the producer will always rule the consumer.

Why don't you start cooking something today? After you have caught your game, make it ready; kill it, wash it, clean it, season it, and then carefully prepare it.

An unused talent is a wasted talent. The master will require from us the profit of the business. We will be called to account for the use of our God-given talent. Ignorance about what to do with it will not be excused and can be expensive. So we need to find out what is in the garden and start making proper use of it.

"Again, the Kingdom of Heaven can be illustrated by the story of a man going on a trip. He called together his servants and gave them money to invest for him while he was gone. He gave five bags of gold to one, two bags of gold to another and one bag of gold to the last – dividing it in proportion to their abilities-and then left on his trip. The servant who received the five bags of gold began immediately to invest the money and soon doubled it. The servant with two bags of gold also went right to work and doubled the money. But the servant who received the one bag of gold dug a hole in the ground and hid the master's money for safekeeping. "After a long time their master returned from his trip and called them to give an account of how they had used his money. The servant to whom he had entrusted the five bags of gold said, `Sir, you gave me five bags of gold to invest, and I have doubled the amount.' The master was full of praise. `Well done, my good and faithful servant. You have been faithful in handling this small amount, so now I will give you many more responsibilities. Let's celebrate together!' "Next came the servant who had received the two bags of gold, with the report, `Sir, you gave me two bags of gold to invest, and I have doubled the amount.' The master said, `Well done, my good and faithful servant. You have been faithful in handling

this small amount, so now I will give you many more responsibilities. Let's celebrate together!' "Then the servant with the one bag of gold came and said, `Sir, I know you are a hard man, harvesting crops you didn't plant and gathering crops you didn't cultivate. I was afraid I would lose your money, so I hid it in the earth and here it is.' "But the master replied, `You wicked and lazy servant! You think I'm a hard man, do you, harvesting crops I didn't plant and gathering crops I didn't cultivate? Well, you should at least have put my money into the bank so I could have some interest. Take the money from this servant and give it to the one with the ten bags of gold. To those who use well what they are given, even more will be given, and they will have an abundance. But from those who are unfaithful, even what little they have will be taken away. Now throw this useless servant into outer darkness, where there will be weeping and gnashing of teeth'" (Matthew 25:14-30, NLT).

Bette Nesmith had a fantastic secretarial job in a Dallas bank when she ran across a problem that interested her. Wasn't there a better way to correct the errors she made on her electric typewriter? Bette had some art experience and she knew that artists who worked in oils just painted over their errors. Maybe that would work for her too. So she concocted a liquid to gloss over her typing errors. Before long, all the secretaries in her building were using what she then had called "Mistake Out." She attempted to sell the product idea to marketing agencies and various companies (including IBM), but they turned her down. However, secretaries continued to use her product. So Bette Nesmith's kitchen became her first manufacturing facility and she started selling it from home. When Bette Nesmith sold the business, the tiny white bottles (containing the liquid paper) were earning £2.18m annually on sales of £23.71m. The buyer was Gillette Company and the sale price was £29.64m.

Do not bury your talent even in the face of opposition. Cook something.

Cook Something Unique And Special

Make something original, different, and unique - something that stands out. It is assumed that Jacob had more than one type of stew. That was why Esau said he wanted "the same red stew." The red stew stood out, if only for its colour.

The reason why we would find KFC next to McDonalds and Burger King is this: they have their individual selling points. They all sell fast food but have their unique selling points (USP). You need to find your strong point and explore it to the maximum.

A talented sales person knows something about everything and everything about something. Why should I come to you if you sell exactly the same product, at the same price as the store next door? There must be something you do differently from the other person.

Here is wisdom. If you sell the same gift item as the shop next door, why don't you encourage your customers to buy their wrapping paper from you and you throw in free wrapping? Do something different.

God has given each person a specific skill or talent; an endowment different from others, but most people die a substandard copy of a warped original. At best you can be a better copy of a good original, but you are still a copy.

When she was young, Florence Chadwick wanted desperately to be a top speed swimmer. At the age of six, she persuaded her parents to enter her in a 50-yard race. She came in last, so she practiced every day for the New Year. Again she entered and lost. When she was an 11-year old, Florence won attention and praise for completing the San Diego Bay endurance swim – 6 miles in all. But she still wanted to be a speed swimmer. At 14, she tried for the National Backstroke Championship but came in second to the famed Eleanor Holm. At 18, she tried out for Olympic speed swimming and came in fourth – only three made the team. Frustrated, she gave it up, married, and moved on to other interests. As she matured, however, Florence began to wonder if she might not have done better if she had specialised in endurance swimming; something that came more naturally. With the help of her father, she began swimming distances again. Twelve years after she had failed to make the Olympic team, Florence Chadwick swam the English Channel in both directions, breaking Gertrude Ederle's 24-year-old record. It took a little time, but eventually she found out what she could do best and did it.

Until Florence settled for her originality, she was frustrated trying to be someone or something she was not made to be.

What About Packaging?

'Red' can also denote packaging; eye catching packaging. We discussed earlier about the colour red in the fourth chapter. One of the things we said was that it whets the appetite. It says 'come and get me.'

Many brilliant ideas are buried in poor packaging. Award winning novels, songs, drama and the likes have ended up in notebooks and collecting dust on shelves because of poor packaging. It is like putting an expensive diamond ring inside a plastic bag and leaving it outside in the front garden. It would remain there for years until someone inadvertently opens the bag or kicks the bag and the gem fly out.

As a bookseller, I have noticed on several occasions that what draws people's attention to a book first of all is the cover, then the title. I know a lot of excellent books that lie on the shelf untouched for some time because they are not imposing on the outside. Therefore, to encourage people to get the books, we tell them "don't judge a book by its cover." That in itself is a subtle admission that the book cover is hideous.

Meet A Need

Do not just 'cook' anything, meet a need. If your product does not meet a need, it will waste. Majority of people I know do not just buy for the sake of it - they want their needs met.

How will you be able to sell cold water or ice cubes to Icelanders or Eskimos? It is just not going to happen. Perhaps with the onset of global warming, things may be different in a few years to come. What point is there in selling winter coats during the summer and selling belly-tops during winter? It just does not make sense.

I have advised Africans not to go into the flower business in a predominantly African community. Some African women may love flowers, but their men do not buy it for them. Most African men do not appreciate flowers. So who in the community is going to buy the perishable flowers? You say, "Maybe God told him to." Really? Maybe He did. Maybe He did not. Have you ever thought this could be a figment of imagination?

It's like someone claiming that God told them to start selling kerosene lantern in the UK? That would be predictive. Except there is a looming catastrophe, kerosene lanterns will not go well in the UK, at least not now.

Whatever you make must meet a need. Don't just do something because you like to. Do something because there is someone out there asking for it. Jacob took advantage of a need in Esau's life. He satisfied Esau's appetite and got his birthright as payment.

Make Profit

Use your product in exchange for what you want. It has been given to you as a means of bargaining. Trade your 'have' for your 'have not.'

Jacob could have given Esau the stew free. But he did not. Instead, he demanded something in exchange. When it comes to your future, nothing else matters, only the birthright will do.

Jacob suddenly remembered his own need and the prophecy upon his life. He either use or lose his opportunity. There was a confusion. To make matters worse, Esau was his twin brother. Would he do it or not? It is all about his future.

Some of us have given out free things we could have traded for our future. Things God gave us for the same purpose – to secure our future.

I knew a dear friend who loved taking photos at functions. He developed the films and gave them out free but did not develop the hobby. He was giving away his future. A few years later I was handed a publication that had the shot of the brother and his family on the front cover. The photo was taken in a studio. It was a session for which he paid hundreds of pounds to the studio. The studio now uses his family photographs for their business promotion without paying them any royalty. I caught up with him then and said to him, 'that studio could have been yours.'

He was using his tool as a toy and was giving out his future free of charge, a little at a time. It is good to help people, but if you do not draw a line, the same people you are helping will take advantage of you and blame you later for being Mr Nice Guy.

Chapter 9

DEAL OR NO DEAL?

Three nights before, Esau noticed he was running low on fresh meat. The stock was only going to take him another day. He therefore went into the woods the next morning but came away with nothing. His failure to catch a game (dead or alive) gave him some concern; he would not have any provisions for his steak tomorrow. The following day was not unusual. Still he had no meat. He had to summon a lot of courage and tried to maintain some kind of sanity and focus. He went to bed that night knowing that there was not going to be any meat for another day except he went to the woods again. He got his bow ready and arrows poisoned before he would eventually go to sleep, making sure everything he would need was all properly assembled and safe inside his quiver. He did not want to allow any delays in the morning; the animals would not be waiting. He would have worn his belt to bed had it not been for the discomfort he was going to suffer during sleep. He determined that another day was not going to go by before he replenishes his meat supply. Going another day without stew was not an option.

Having left so early, Esau had hoped to return home well before lunch, so he did not have breakfast or prepare any sandwich for the journey. "Today is going to be a different day," he thought to himself. Hours passed and still no wandering deer. No buffalo, no stray lamb. Not even a small snake whistle were heard. As a good hunter who knew his job quite well, Esau changed his tactics. Instead of waiting for the animals while he hid in the clefts of the rocks, he went straight to the brooks where they normally would gather together to drink. As if it was a game plan, the animals did not visit the brook while Esau was there. Frustrated, Esau started to pull himself home when he suddenly heard the rustle of the trees and saw what appeared to be a large animal flying past. He swiftly got out his arrows, took position and had a second look at the animal. Though Esau's face was a little dreary, he pretended he was fine, summoned the little strength he had left, took a deep breath and as he got ready to launch his arrow, the animal appeared in full view from within the thick of the bush. To his greatest disappointment, it was a pig. Pig? What would a Hebrew boy do with a pig?

As Esau turned his back to finally leave, he noticed a fox being pursued by a lion. In a split second, he had a decision to make. Should he allow the lion to kill the fox being a resident of the bush with a good knowledge of the terrain? Afterwards, he would kill the lion and then take his game. Or should he otherwise go after the fox and secure his game and then risk the attack of a hungry and ferocious lion? Esau decided to go after the lion, firing a few arrows at it in rapid succession getting rid of it before the fox could get any refuge in the holes. At long last Esau got a game; the fox could not escape his ability. Now extremely tired and famished, he struggled to get the little fox out of the woods and started his journey back home.

Barely stepping his foot into the house door, Esau shouted in a voice that sounded overarching, "Hey bruv, what's happening?"

"Not a lot," replied Jacob from the back room. "I've been so busy in the kitchen. I'm only just sitting down to relax since you left in the morning."

"Man, I'm tired too. Do you have anything on offer?"

"Offer? No, no, just some stew."

Off went Jacob to get the stew.

Knowing getting the stew would have been the usual reaction of his brother, Esau added, "Hey Jay! That same red one, remember?"

As if to be abruptly interrupted in his track, Jacob rushed back to confirm his brother's request. "Did I just hear you mention the red one?"

"Yeah, the same red one I enjoy the most."

"You must be joking."

"Nope, I may be tired, but, not of the red stew."

Jacob's next response would seem to be premeditated. Yet without thinking, he responded quickly, "That's not on offer, don't even try." He had no intention of giving away part of the meal he had so tirelessly been cooking just like that, not without an exchange.

Knowing he could not get the red stew without a fight, Esau now made an offer. "You can have my clothes, sandals, bow, arrows … anything you want."

"Really, anything I want?"

"Sure, you can have anything, even the birthright."

Jacob's eyes lit up. At last, he can get hold on the much coveted birthright. They had spoken about it before but the chances of ever obtaining it was naught. He thought to himself, 'let me get the birthright first, and I can fight for the blessing later." He rushed back in to get the red stew and returned immediately.

Stopping right at Esau's face, Jacob cleared his throat, "Ugh, ugh, did you say I can have your birthright if I want?"

"Oh please, is that not enough?" replied Esau.

"Sorry, just checking. But just to be sure, can I have it today?"

With the stew in sight and the smell overpowering, Esau mumbled within himself whether he should withdraw the offer and go without food for a couple of hours. Suddenly, his empty stomach began to rumble and churn and his taste buds ignited. Esau could no longer resist the sight of the red colour of the stew. He wouldn't miss it for anything.

Noticing the emotional confusion in his brother, Jacob decided to break the long silence, "Deal or no deal?"

"Deal. What is the birthright to me anyway since I'm about to die?"

Esau sold his birthright for a morsel of stew. He sold his future. Don't sell your future. Don't make a deal with the world.

> "Stop loving this evil world and all that it offers you, for when you love the world, you show that you do not have the love of the Father in you. For the world offers only the lust for physical pleasure, the lust for everything we see, and pride in our possessions. These are not from the Father. They are from this evil world.

And this world is fading away, along with everything it craves. But if you do the will of God, you will live forever" (I John 2:15-17, NLT).

Jacob Versus Esau

It is easy to lay all the blame on Esau or even Jacob but who are these guys?

"When the boys grew up, Esau became a skilful hunter, a man of the field, but Jacob was a peaceful man (plain man, KJV), living in tents" (Genesis 25:27, NASB).

Godly Jacob

It is rather unfortunate that the pictures painted by many translators of the Bible and honest preachers including myself for many years has poisoned the minds of thousands and perhaps millions toward such a delightful character in the person of Jacob. It is a picture of a trickster, a cunning, dubious, and dangerous fraudster. He is even described as a supplanter.

However, Jacob was extremely hospitable, kind, caring, godly, peaceful, honest, hard-working, and fair, a loving father, and a faithful husband. Space will not allow me to expound on these qualities in this book. It is a subject worth exploring in another book. This same sentiment is captured in one of the writings of Chuck Smith.

Now I'm afraid that the translators have done Jacob an unfortunate turn in translating this "a plain man." The word that they translated was the Hebrew word "tam." It was translated "plain." The word in other places in the Old Testament have been translated "perfect." You remember when God said to Satan concerning Job "Have you considered my servant Job, a 'perfect' man?" That's the same Hebrew word, "tam." Concerning Job, it was translated "perfect." And so the translators have done Jacob kind of a bad turn, calling him a plain man. The scripture is actually saying he was a perfect man, or a complete man, but he dwelt in tents.

Now we have a tendency to actually put Jacob down, and I have to admit that I have done my share of putting this guy down because of some of the tricks he pulled. But, in reality, he was the guy that God had chosen. And the fascinating thing is that God never put him down.

The last time I put him down, the Lord spoke to me and said "Hey, how come you keep putting him down?" I said, "Oh man, look at those horrible things he did." He said "Hey, where did I put him down?" And I looked, and I could not find where God put Jacob down, so I quit putting Jacob down.

Jacob was not evil, he was shrewd. What about Esau?

Ungodly Esau

Esau was hugely flippant about the birthright. He said to Jacob "Hey man, what about the birthright? I'm ready to die; I want your pottage."

So Jacob pressed the point in and said, "Swear to me then this day;" and he swore to him: and so he sold his birthright to Jacob. Then Jacob gave Esau the bread and the pottage of lentils; which he did eat and drink, and they rose up, and he rose up and went his way: thus Esau despised his birthright.

He didn't actually care about the birthright at all. He wasn't interested in spiritual things. He could care less about his birthright. He hated it; he wasn't interested in it. And therefore he despised his birthright. No wonder God described him as godless.

> *"See that no one is sexually immoral, or is godless like Esau, who for a single meal sold his inheritance rights as the oldest son. Afterward, as you know, when he wanted to inherit this blessing, he was rejected. He could bring about no change of mind, though he sought the blessing with tears"* *(Hebrews 12:16-17, NIV).*

What Esau had by providence, Jacob acquired by promise and prudence. Things you may not have by providence, you can get through promise, prayer and prudence. God may have promised you a million things and can sovereignly bring them to pass in your life, but by demonstrating prudence they are released to you. If you miss the opportunities God brings your way, you may pay for them dearly in the future.

Jacob would not wait another day to seize the moment. He would later get the blessing but "Now," he said, "is the time for the birthright."

Materials Consulted

1. Adaptation of Dr. George Sweetings Special Sermons for Special Days.
2. Bits & Pieces, April 4, 1991.
3. Bits & Pieces, June, 1990, pp. 23-24.
4. Bits & Pieces, March 3, 1994, p. 7.
5. Bits and Pieces, Vol. F, #41.
6. Chuck Smith, Senior Pastor of Calvary Chapel, Atlanta, Georgia USA
7. Crossroads, Issue No. 7, p. 9.
8. Crossroads, Issue No. 7, pp. 3-4.
9. Dave Wilkenson
10. David McCullough, Mornings on Horseback.
11. Denis Waitley in The Winner's Edge (Berkley Books) quoted in Bits & Pieces, March 4, 1993, p. 13-15.
12. Discipleship Journal, #48, p. 33.
13. Dr. Jimmy Allen, former pastor of First Baptist Church, San Antonio, Texas in Pulpit Helps, May, 1991.
14. From "Present Day Parables" by J. Wilbur Chapman.
15. Harold Kellock, Houdini.
16. http://www.who.int/genomics/public/geneticdiseases/en/index2.html
17. Lee Shayne, T. D. Jakes: America's New Preacher (New York: New York University Press, 2005), pp. 33-60.
18. Moody's Anecdotes, pp. 48-49.
19. Our Daily Bread
20. Today in the Word, Moody Bible Institute, August, 1990.
21. Today in the Word, Moody Bible Institute, January, 1992, p. 10.
22. Today in the Word, Moody Bible Institute, October, 1991, p. 18.
23. Walk Through Rewards.
24. www.forbes.com/billionaires October 5, 2012.

www.ingramcontent.com/pod-product-compliance
Lightning Source LLC
Chambersburg PA
CBHW051952090426
42741CB00008B/1361